The New Nationalism

Pergamon Titles of Related Interest

PERGAMON
POLICY
STUDIES

The New Nationalism
Implications for Transatlantic Relations

Edited by
Werner Link
Werner J. Feld

Pergamon Press
NEW YORK • OXFORD • TORONTO • SYDNEY • FRANKFURT • PARIS

Pergamon Press Offices:

U.S.A.   Pergamon Press Inc., Maxwell House, Fairview Park,
                  Elmsford, New York 10523, U.S.A.

U.K.   Pergamon Press Ltd., Headington Hill Hall,
                  Oxford OX3 0BW, England

CANADA   Pergamon of Canada, Ltd., 75 The East Mall,
                  Toronto, Ontario M8Z 5W3, Canada

AUSTRALIA   Pergamon Press (Aust) Pty. Ltd., P O Box 544,
                  Potts Point, NSW 2011, Australia

FRANCE   Pergamon Press SARL, 24 rue des Ecoles,
                  75240 Paris, Cedex 05, France

FEDERAL REPUBLIC   Pergamon Press GmbH, 6242 Kronberg/Taunus,
OF GERMANY   Pferdstrasse 1, Federal Republic of Germany

Library of Congress Cataloging in Publication Data

Committee on Atlantic Studies.
   The new nationalism.

   (Pergamon policy studies)
   1. North Atlantic region--Politics and govern-
ment--Congresses. 2. Nationalism--North Atlantic
region--Congresses. I. Link, Werner. II. Feld,
Werner, J. III. Title.
D839.2.C63 1978   320.5'4'091821   78-17144
ISBN 0-08-023370-8
ISBN 0-08-023369-4 pbk.

Printed in the United States of America

Contents

THE NEW NATIONALISM
AND SUB-NATIONAL REGIONALISM

Foreword

It is not always easy to take a number of papers, no matter how excellent, that were given at an international conference and transfer them into a book. However, our task as editors was eased considerably by two factors: the careful selection of topics and guidelines for the prospective authors, and the willingness of the authors to revise their manuscripts. Whatever editing was necessary for those manuscripts contributed in a language other than English has been kept to a minimum. Professor Guy Héraud's paper was written in French and was translated through the good offices of Charles R. Foster, Executive Secretary of the Committee on Atlantic Studies.

We would like to express our deep gratitude to Mr. Foster for his tireless efforts on behalf of the Luxembourg Conference and the CAS in general; to Mr. Werner Doerr, Assistant to Professor Link at the University of Trier, for the circumspect preparations in setting up the conference in Luxembourg; and last, but not least, to Mrs. Jan Davis of the Department of Political Science at the University of New Orleans for her excellent counsel and assistance in putting the finishing touches to the manuscript.

Werner Link
Werner Feld
Editors

Trier and New Orleans
March 1978

Acknowledgements

This volume presents a collection of papers given at the Annual Conference of the Committee on Atlantic Studies held in Luxembourg on September 23 and 24, 1977. The conference was made possible by a generous grant from the Thyssen Foundation in Dusseldorf, Germany. Additional financial assistance was given by the United States Embassy in Bonn, the United States Mission to the European Community, and NATO. We are greatly indebted to these institutions and wish to express our appreciation to all those who helped organize the conference and publish its findings.

The Committee on Atlantic Studies

Werner J. Feld   Werner Link
Chairman, North America   Chairman, Europe

Charles R. Foster
Executive Secretary

The Committee on Atlantic Studies was organized in the United States and Canada in 1964 and merged with a similar European group in 1967. The North American and European sections of the Committee consist of some fifty university professors and scholars who meet as a full Committee annually. Its purpose is to foster collaboration and contacts within the educational community, such as the organization in colleges and universities of seminars for both faculty and student discussions. A transatlantic dialogue is fostered through such meetings, which also serve as a vehicle for the publication of original contributions such as this volume. The Committee is affiliated with the Atlantic Council of the United States and the Atlantic Institute, Paris.

1 Introduction
Werner Link

Nationalism and New Nationalism have become catchwords with many different meanings which political scientists and others have analyzed from various perspectives. Many authors have described and interpreted at length the origins and development of classical nationalism, while others have devoted more attention to the nationalism of developing countries. Up until now, however, the New Nationalism in the advanced industrialized states of the Western world and its impact on their relations in the Atlantic area have attracted little interest. This volume is designed to help fill that gap by clarifying the concept of New Nationalism, analyzing the situation to which it refers, and suggesting political procedures to cope with the difficult problems it involves.

It may be of assistance to the reader to know that the outline sent to all participants of the CAS Conference - to the authors of the following papers as well as to the discussants - began with a working hypothesis taken from Theodore Geiger's book, The Fortunes of the West: The Future of the Atlantic Nations (Indiana University Press, 1973). New Nationalism was tentatively understood as that reorientation toward national welfare which has resulted from three international trends:

(1) the expanding size and diversity of national aims (i.e., the maintenance of economic growth and full employment, the continuing improvement of living standards, the equitable distribution of income, the conservation of natural and man-made environments, the advancement of knowledge, the safeguarding of national security and the meeting of international responsibility);

(2) the increasing politicalization of the process of resource allocation;

(3) the growing importance of the agencies and activities of national governments.

New Nationalism is characterized, therefore, by the manner in which the governments of Western industrialized countries give top priority to national objectives and processes, putting them before foreign relations and international commitments. Contrary to classical nationalism, which is usually of an aggressive nature, the policy adopted by New Nationalism tends to be rather defensive and inward-looking in character. Self-satisfaction and the desire to enjoy the fruits of industrial progress have replaced nationalistic emotions. Apparently the device of New Nationalism is exclusiveness rather than expansion.

The continuously growing demands on national governments contrast sharply with the development toward a globalization of socio-economic problems. Nations are now being confronted with global socio-economic interdependencies demanding global political answers, and national governments are being forced to adopt policies which are more conducive to international coordination. However, international attempts to achieve such cooperation (for example, the summit conferences in Rambouillet, Puerto Rico, and London) are not initiated with the aim of surrendering national functions or shifting them to a supranational level, but with the intention of improving the "national situation" (Stanley Hoffman). There is, then, a contradictory and ambivalent relationship between the unilateral pursuit of national welfare objectives and the attempted coordination under conditions of interdependence.

The conference papers published in this volume test the analytical validity of the concept of New Nationalism; they confront tentative propositions with empirical evidence at different interaction levels; they clarify the domestic and international condition of New Nationalism and analyze its impact on the political and economic fields of the Atlantic nations. There emerges a sophisticated picture of an extremely complicated phenomenon - "a coherent syndrome of psychological, structural, behavioral and institutional factors which seem endemic to the historical development of industrial society" (Caporaso). National governments enjoy increasing international interdependence, yet fear it because of the uncertainty of its outcome. International interdependence offers opportunities for unprecedented gain, but is, at the same time, a source of vulnerability. The internationalization of production, the international division of labor, and transnational processes are also accompanied by the internationalization of internal struggles and the export of domestic problems. Conversely, international politics become "domesticated" (Hanrieder). New Nationalism, according to James Caporaso, is "inward-looking" with respect to aims and "outward-looking" with respect to means. This means that the processes of redistribution which traditionally characterize the domestic struggle between classes and social groups increasingly determine the processes of international politics. This new type of international politics does not adversely affect the nation-state; it simply means that the pursuit of national interest is oriented less and less toward the traditional values of prestige, territorial security, and expansion. "Non-distributive political processes are giving way to distributive processes expressed largely in economic terms" (Hanrieder). Economic security becomes the main aim of the nation state in accordance with the expectations of its citizens and its competing domestic groups.

The question of whether this development described as New Nationalism is merely a series of short-term peripheral changes or whether it represents a long-term fundamental reorientation of Western society in the sense of a secular trend is explored thoroughly in the various papers; the answer favors the second alternative. The individual authors chose to differ only on the question of when this fundamental reorientation actually began:

(a) If one views modern socialism, total war and the Great Depression of the 1930s as the three progenitors of the social dimension now evident in foreign policy, the shift in the order of priority from the political and strategic aims of modern governments in their external policies to predominately economic and social objectives is assumed to have already occurred in the immediate post-war years (Northedge).

(b) If one views developments in a global political power context, then New Nationalism is primarily an expression of rational calculations on "how to further national interest within a global configuration of power (and its regional manifestations) in which the superpowers exerted an overwhelming measure of influence" (Hanrieder).

(c) Viewed from the world-wide economic angle, the change from expanding economy to a universal recession and stagflation becomes the turning point; in this case we must regard the 1970s as the beginning of New Nationalism (Morse, Goldstein).

If one pursues the last two hypotheses, then the erosion of America's role as a leading power, both politically and economically, is the concrete reason for neo-nationalistic reorientation (Morse). New Nationalism is then, in essense, reactive behavior by nation states to the change in the international configuration where no superpower makes the rules or directs its efforts toward the agreement and enforcement of international rules. Interpreted on the basis of system analysis, New Nationalism can be explained as a phenomenon arising from the conditions created by a system-dominance which could well determine the course of the last third of this century (Goldstein).

Just how the essential coordination can be achieved under such conditions (the secular trend toward reorientation of national societies with concomitant interdependence and system-dominance) is the main tenor of the majority of the papers. After World War II the United States, on the strength of its hegemonial position and its ability to make dollar loans available, brought about coordination on the global level within the terms of the Bretton Woods System and on the regional level through the European Recovery Program. Nowadays both the coordination and the "oil" for the coordinating machinery are lacking (Morse). The old and the new forums of international discussion and coordination are now primarily used by countries to exert influence on the internal and economic policies of the participating states. In other words, attempts at coordination are being undertaken in the service of neo-nationalistic politics in order to exercise control over interdependence. The national interests still govern as efforts are made to solve at least some of the problems which have arisen as a result of internationalization of production, exchange processes, and communication. In this respect, it has become apparent that national governments have very little room to maneuver.

In some Atlantic states ethnic independence movements have emerged, further impeding the coordinating capabilities of national governments externally and internally. Because of its increasing importance, this phenomenon is dealt with in separate chapters in this book. The cases of Quebec and Scotland, in particular, demonstrate the specific links between New Nationalism and ethnic nationalism (Soldatos, Foster). Whether federalism will permanently resolve the main problems of ethnic nationalism, as Heraud supposes, remains an open question.

In view of the countless difficulties which are discussed in the individual papers, the prospects for successful coordination under neo-nationalistic conditions are deemed to be rather gloomy. Unilateralism is not only a threatening alternative; it frequently determines actual behavior (Czempiel). In the opinion of many authors neo-mercantilistic thinking is characteristic of the current situation in which zero-sum games with negative outcomes for all govern international politics (Goldstein). Whereas back in the 1950s and 1960s integration was viewed as the objective of internal European and transatlantic policy, coordination has now become a substitute for integration - located about halfway between the two extremes of divergence and integration (Hanrieder). Even this modest development tends, in practice, to result in negative cooperation achieving perhaps agreement on targets (Morse). Only at the lowest level of coordination, "problem search and definition" or agreement on removal of obstacles, does there seem to be some chance of success in the near future (Morse). Whether as a result of the pressure of demands by the developing countries - similar to the pressure of the Soviet Union and the threat perceived by the Western countries in the late 1940s - coordination can be achieved more easily in the future, or whether the differences between the industrialized nations will be aggravated, remains an open question (Northedge). In order to be able to move from "problem search" to coordination at a higher level, to a harmonization and standardization of national responses, a more accurate definition of interdependence is needed. A concept of interaction has to be developed which reflects the existing degree of both interdependence and independence in the various state groupings and which recognizes specific problem areas (Czempiel).

In the final analysis, of course, political coordination cannot be brought about by clarifying analytical concepts or by defining situations. It requires political will and engagement to manage international interdependence. Who is expected to do that? Since one single coordinator is unlikely to emerge in the near future, there is no alternative but collective consensus-building and negotiating processes. This is not only the task of governments but even more that of non-governmental societal groups and organizations which have transatlantic links. What has been stated theoretically about the management of potentially turbulent systems in general can be applied to the specific case of the present turbulent international system: "Because there are no externally prescribed guidelines, they have to be worked out collaboratively. Institutionalization of organizations in terms of shared values plays a vital role in giving form and context to the resultant networks of overlapping social controls established in the areas of functional interdependence. As Sherif has pointed out, recognition and acceptance of the fact of functional interdependence creates a sense of 'common predicament' and promotes the search for superordinated goals. Superordinate goals are not eternal truths, but development hypotheses about what constitutes a sufficient basis for inter-group cooperation. Network organizations have an important role to play in providing a continuing focus for the collaborative resolution of collective problems."*

If this volume stimulates further search for superordinate goals in the Atlantic area and strengthens transatlantic links and networks, then it will have attained its foremost objective.

---

* J.L. Metcalfe, "System Models, Economic Models and the Causal Texture of Organizational Environment: An Approach to Macro-Organization Theory." Human Relations, vol. 27 (1974) pp. 658-9.

2 What is the New Nationalism or Is There a New Nationalism?
James Caporaso

"The traditional agenda of international affairs - the balance among major powers, the security of nations - no longer defines our perils or our possibilities. To some extent we have mastered many of the familiar challenges of diplomacy. Yet suddenly we are witnessing a new threat to the governability of national societies and to the structure of international stability. A crisis threatens the world's economic system." (1)

INTRODUCTION

What is the New Nationalism and what role does this phenomenon play in the contemporary political economy of the Atlantic World? (2) This is the question I was charged with addressing in preparing this paper. My unease concerning the assumption contained in the question - that a new category of analysis is represented by the term New Nationalism - led me to append the subquestion, "Or is there a New Nationalism?" I do not wish to quibble over the fine points of distinguishing what is old and what is new. I am concerned only that this term, should it be adopted, adds not only an extra word but also a new category of analysis. A good definition should set out the properties that draw a set of phenomena together as well as the characteristics that serve to distinguish them from other phenomena. Political scientists, even those interested in "getting on" with concrete investigations, are not immune to the rules of good definitions.

DEFINITIONS

According to the Dean of the study of nationalism, Hans Kohn, "nationalism is a state of mind in which the supreme loyalty of the individual is felt to be due the nation-state." (3) For Karl Deutsch, a nation, or a people, is "a community of shared meanings, or, more broadly still, a group of people who have interlocking habits of communication." (4) Both scholars stress the importance of nationalism as a coherent set of meanings, but Kohn is more strongly identified with the importance of nationally oriented attitudes and "feelings" of loyalty to the national group while Deutsch stresses the transactional and behavioral components of nationalism. In Deutsch's cybernetic language, shared meanings and common symbols are important primarily because they allow one to "decode" the actions of others, hence enabling one to predict the behavior of others and to be responsive to it. A shared culture, a common language, and similar social cues become particularly crucial in that they facilitate the exchange of informaton and the comprehension of the intentions, and hence the purposive actions, of others.

Though Professors Kohn and Deutsch differ in the importance they attach to attitudes and loyalties, both seem to be in agreement in relegating the state to a positon of the dependent variable in the twin processes of state and nation formation. Kohn treats the process of the formation of the state as the end result of a protracted struggle of a group to effectively exert its identity and to realize its idea of nationalism in an autonomous set of political institutions. In a similar vein, Deutsch places great stock in the importance of voluntary groups, social homogeneity, and the transactional cohesion reflected in the web of flows cutting across various territorial groups. In fact, to push the argument further with a metaphor, Deutsch's approach to the question of nationalism suggests a "tearsheet" notion of nations, a series of naturally coherent groupings. The role of the state in shaping, tampering, and coercing the outlines of the nation is not stressed.

Without extending our definitional search beyond these two eminent scholars, we begin to see that nationalism is not a single variable that can be described in terms of a series of gradations along one continuum but a cluster of more or less distinct traits that cohere in ideal-typical fashion. That is, we not only talk about how strong or weak nationalism is in a particular location in our globe, but we also speak of what particular form it assumes, suggesting qualitative as well as quantitative changes. We need only think of the proliferation of terms to demonstrate this: liberal nationalism, Jacobin nationalism, integral nationalism, ethnic nationalism, separatist nationalism, cultural nationalism, and militant nationalism, to name only a few. These are distinct types of nationalism representing different clusters of variables, not merely different gradations of intensity of a single nationalism.

This orientation leads naturally to the guiding question of this paper: what is the New Nationalism? According to Theodore Geiger, the New Nationalism involves a reorientation of national feelings, attention and resources toward internal (domestic) considerations and a commensurate decrease in bellicose, xenophobic nationalism that characterized the nineteenth and early twentieth centuries. (5) Paralleling the shift mirrored by Kissinger in the opening quotation, the transition to the New Nationalism involves a shift from questions of defense, security, and diplomacy to those concerned with solving the economic problems of advanced industrial societies: maintenance of economic growth and full employment, improvement of quality of life, management of inflation, pollution, and a host of other similar problems. Since these problems are seen as primarily domestic, one suspects a turning inward in several senses. There is less need to cooperate with international institutions, greater attention to domestic policy-making, and a heightened role for those portions of the state, whether they be legislative, administrative, executive, or party, that have primary responsibility for the making of foreign policy. (6) This reorientation of domestic-international priorities in favor of the domestic is seen as a benign move, a mild form of isolationism, and certainly not an aggressive, outward-oriented feeling. That in itself would seem to argue for more pacific, if less active, transatlantic relations.

Thus the transition of the New Nationalism comprehends a syndrome of three interrelated characteristics. There is a movement from international to domestic preoccupations, including both an attitudinal shift toward neoisolationist sentiments and a structural change toward a new emphasis on domestic priorities and programs. Secondly, the transition to the New Nationalism involves a shift of emphasis from warfare to welfare, from the bellicose to the pacific, and from the economic to the political - all of which can perhaps be summarized in the notion of the triumph of low politics over high politics. Thirdly, the New Nationalism involves a new acceleration of political demands, albeit low-political demands, made by an increasingly mobilized citizenry. Thus the term New Nationalism serves at once as a summary label for a strong dose of economic materialism, combined with hints of an "end of ideology" at the cultural level, along with a belief in the historical impact of long-term trends inherent in the modernization of society. Though the forces enventually producing the New Nationalism have been gestating for a long time, it was not until the mid-1960s that this form of nationalism came into existence. (7)   The catalyzing factors were the hardening of the Cold War or the moderation of this Cold War into a period of competitive coexistence, the consolidation of the success of the European Economic Community (EEC) centering on the achievement of a common agricultural policy, and the sharp increases in welfare expenditures in the United States.

THEORETICAL IMPLICATIONS

What are some of the implications of the trend toward the New Nationalism? Clearly, this phenomenon is an important one whose spokesmen see it as part of a long-term, fundamental reorientation of Western society, and not as a series of short-term changes at the margins. I believe the following things should occur, or should have occurred, if the theoretical underpinnings of the New Nationalism are on solid ground:

(1) An increasing share of the national budget should be going to domestic concerns, and these concerns should be characterized by welfare-oriented economic goals (as a result of the increased importance of the low-political sector).

(2) An increasing share of public expenditures over gross national product (following from the mobilization hypothesis).

(3) As a correlate of number 2, we should find an increasing politicization of economic policy in the sense of state involvement in economic life and in decisions about the production and distribution of goods and resources. To the extent that society's economy becomes internationalized, there should be an increasing international role for domestic political institutions.

(4) A decreasing share of the national budget should be dedicated to defense and security concerns due to the decline in high politics hypothesis.

(5) There should be changing cleavage patterns in the mass electorate

with the "axial principles" defining loyalties to parties, as well as the patterns of divisions among them, changing to reflect the post-industrial concerns of worker, employee, technocrat, and civil servant.   Whether a decline of ideology will occur as part of this, or merely a recasting of the axes which define the ideology, is something which the concept of New Nationalism does not tell us.

(6) At the level of public opinion, an increased salience of domestic objectives should be observed.   Part of this change in priorities should be due to a reallocation of attention, on the part of both the masses and the elites, away from international objectives toward domestic ones.   Another part of the increased salience of domestic objectives should be due to the incorporation of individuals who were previously politically quiescent into the political system.   So there are two components of the increased importance of domestic objectives, one a shift or redistribution of priorities, the other a growth in the source of political demands.

I will not claim that all of these important developments follow rigorously from a single theoretical position.   Indeed, many additional assumptions are made by advocates of the New Nationalism in order to reach these conclusions.   However, there is a basic, core idea here and I believe it centers around the idea of modernization (thought of in Morse's sense), and the inexorable growth of functional rationality, i.e., the development of more and more efficient techniques and technologies for solving concrete problems.   At the mass level this view sees ideological cleavages between workers and employees as becoming progressively less important, along with a corresponding diminution in the importance of cleavages centering on communities of sentiment, such as ethnic groups.   At the elite level we find heroic leadership giving way to the economic manager: D'Estaing, Schmidt, and Brezhnev have replaced earlier post-war leaders deGaulle, Adenauer, and Khrushchev. Whether the revolution of modernization is inherently inward-looking in the sense of providing the long-term forces which produce an inward orientation, an economic nationalism à la Sombart, or an anti-cosmopolitanism is difficult to say.   Similarly, whether it makes any sense at all to talk about a post-modern personality, if by that we mean a coherent set of psychological traits rooted in historical forces, is very controversial. (8) However, what we can observe with certainty is that more and more of the public budget is allocated for non-military concerns as a greater number of individuals are brought inside the political system.

As to the decline in defense expenditures, at least relative to gross national product, a number of different arguments are possible.   However, there is very little we can say about the relationship between modernization and defense spending per se.   It is true that defense spending as a share of GNP has levelled off and declined in the 1960s and 1970s, but it is difficult to determine if this decline represents a long-term secular trend or a more historically specific phenomenon.   For example, the decrease in military expenditures among advanced industrial societies might reflect the declining utility of military forces in the current strategic era, an era characterized by the reluctance of leaders to run the escalatory risks implicit in using sub-nuclear weapons. As Morse has argued:

... the policy-making elite of the super-powers became socialized into a world of nuclear weaponry and for practical purposes has by and large accepted the stalemate at the nuclear level. This has meant that plays for power and position, which once took place with intimations of the use of force, now more frequently occur when states adjust their economic positions to one another. (9)

This strategic deadlock, along with historical factors which persuaded many Western European countries to default part of their national defense to the United States, led many scholars to speak of the declining utility of force in the contemporary international system. To the extent that the premises of this argument are valid, it accounts for the declining defense expenditures as well as the increasing share of welfare objectives in public spending. Indeed, these two phenomena are in part components of a single functional relationship where one often gains at the other's expense, a conclusion superbly demonstrated by Russett's chapter titled "The Opportunity Costs of American Defense." (10) What we should keep in mind is that declining defense expenditures are almost certainly not due to a long-term decline in industrial man's bellicosity. Rather this decline may represent a much shorter-term effect, especially if technologies are developed for carrying on sub-nuclear combat that decreases the fear of escalation.

Finally, we need to direct our attention to a more international role. There are really two separate questions here. The first asks why we expect a movement in the direction of internationalization at all and, indeed, whether this might be inconsistent with our earlier argument about the "turning inward" aspect of the New Nationalism. The second question is, once the argument for internationalism is made, why would we expect the international response to center on the domestic bureaucracies rather than some supranational institution? The answer to the first question is somewhat easier than the second. We would expect a move toward internationalism because it is consistent with the underlying forces of modernization: specialization, mobility of factors of production, standardization of productive forces, exploitation of economies of scale, and taking full advantage of comparative advantages whether they reside in intra-national, international or trans-national units. According to this mode of economic rationality, national frontiers are merely legal impediments that one must remove in order to make full use of the world's resources.

Given an increase in the amount of economic activity internationally, why should we expect an increased role for domestic agencies and institutions in the regulation and implementation of foreign economic policy? Perhaps the answer to this question should be obvious. However, let us think back to less than ten years ago when there was broad agreement among regional integration scholars that it was primarily economic forces that would take us beyond the nation-state and toward supra-national integration. Thus, the progression of the late phase of the Industrial Revolution, the rise of the manager and technocrat to positions of importance in policy-making, the increasing demands on the part of previously politically quiescent groups for the fruits of the service state, the decline of the "night-watchman state" and the rise of the "service state," and the increased importance of specialized knowledge in policy-making, were all part and parcel of the package of social and economic transformations called the "New Europe" almost two decades ago. The present discussion of the New Nationalism sounds very familiar.

Let me offer two hypotheses as to why the political response to the international aspects of modernization will center on domestic institutions. The first hypothesis is that the domestic route assures much greater control by central national institutions and hence is less threatening to them than the process of supra-national integration. However valid this hypothesis may be, I suspect that it injects far too much purpose and foresight into the process by which the internationalization of domestic agencies takes place. The growth of an international function within domestic bureaucracies in the United States took place incrementally, perhaps even haphazardly, with about 60 such agencies having a hand in the conduct of foreign economic policy. (11) This suggests my second hypothesis, that the growth of the international role of domestic bureaucracies (12) is due to the insufficiently developed policy networks linking supra-national institutions to society. That is, there were not sufficient opportunities for domestic groups with a strong interest in international activity to register an impact. It was true that domestic groups could work through national ministries to influence international organizations, but this only provided another layer of bureaucracy between the individual and the focus of decision-making. A more direct route, one likely to maximize the effectiveness of pressure tactics as well as to preserve political control, utilizes domestic institutions.

The trend toward the New Nationalism also has important implications for international relations and the conduct of foreign policy. According to Geiger, since the New Nationalism involves a preoccupation with national objectives, it contrasts to classical nationalism which was "aggressive, expansionist and often xenophobic." (13) However, this turning inward has to be understood in a very special sense. It is a turning inward of goals so that most goals center on needs or interests of groups inside the domestic context. This does not necessarily mean that the means of achieving them are also domestic. On the contrary, since international interdependence has been increasing along with the growing concern for managing domestic economic processes, it follows that the management of these goals will become increasingly internationalized.

In particular, several consequences should follow from the conjunction of increased international involvement and the New Nationalism. First of all, there should be a higher level of interdependence among the nation-states. Were this interdependence to increase only at the rate by which involvement increases, the proposition would be obvious. However, we are saying that, due to the increased scope of political control within national societies, each unit of international involvement will produce greater sensitivity. Second, one would expect to see a greater reliance on economic tools for achieving foreign goals on the assumption that where the means exist they will be used, particularly in light of the declining role of force. Third, one expects to find greater politicization of economic relations among states - perhaps entailing an increased role for tariff and non-tariff barriers to trade - increased adjustment assistance to groups damaged by international economic activity, and the reappearance of protectionist sentiment generally. One expects the re-emergence of protectionism and economic nationalism to flow from some of the forces behind the New Nationalism but not others. The mobilization of individuals into interest groups to press their claims in areas which were once dormant could make foreign economic policy a very controversial area. A textile worker who has lost his job may not be consoled by the economic argument that a nation is better off specializing in what it does best. As more and more groups acquire the right to enter this policy-making sphere, the impact is likely to be more and more protectionist. This is the societal aspect of economic nationalism. On the other hand, I do not believe that economically strong, industrialized countries will actively pursue protectionist policies. States may follow such a policy because of domestic constraints, but it is unlikely they will gain a real long-term advantage from such a foreign policy. And most emphatically, the foregoing is not intended to mean that states will not choose to pursue policies which reduce their dependence, and minimize their vulnerabilities to others. The effort to diversify markets, to search for alternate sources of supply, to avoid the clustering of international economic activity in a few sources, to build stockpiles, and to provide domestic alternatives to goods supplied externally are likely to be popular strategies in the era ahead. But these are distributional questions about the allocation of international activity - not questions directly affecting the size of the international pie.

EMPIRICAL EVIDENCE

The usual disclaimers about empirical evidence not being definitive need to be taken very seriously here. I offer no comprehensive assessment of any of the propositons, but merely attempt to confront these propositions with the broadest and most obvious bodies of evidence available.

The Rise of Public Expenditures

The increase in governmental expenditures, in constant dollars and as a share of GNP, is one of the clearer trends in almost all advanced industrial societies. This appears to be a long-term secular trend which accelerated above its normal growth in the last two decades. Around the turn of the century, the ratio of governmental expenditures to national wealth was between 5% and 10% in many Western countries. (14) Today this proportion has increased to above 30% in most of these countries. In West Germany it is in the 40% area and in Sweden it is in the 50% area. (15) Even in the shorter term we can see significant increases in this trend. In the United States public expenditures as a share of GNP increased from 26.5% in 1954 to 34.2% in 1976. That this reflected more the politicization rather than the nationalization of society is indicated by the fact that the state and local sector increased more rapidly than the federal sector. (16) The growth of both federal and state-local expenditures for the United States is plotted on Chart 1.

The Increase in Welfare Expenditures

The structural increase in public expenditures is, on hypothesis, said to be accompanied by a corresponding increase in welfare-oriented public programs; hence, there should be a rising share of economic-welfare spending as a proportion of total public spending. Edward Morse has provided us with evidence about the growth of welfare-tied public expenses in France from the late nineteenth century to the 1960s. His data demonstrate that welfare expenditures have increased significantly, to a large measure at the expense of defense programs. (17) These expenditure increases occurred in many areas, including higher education, social services, housing, and social security.

CHART I

The Growing Public Sector, 1929-1976

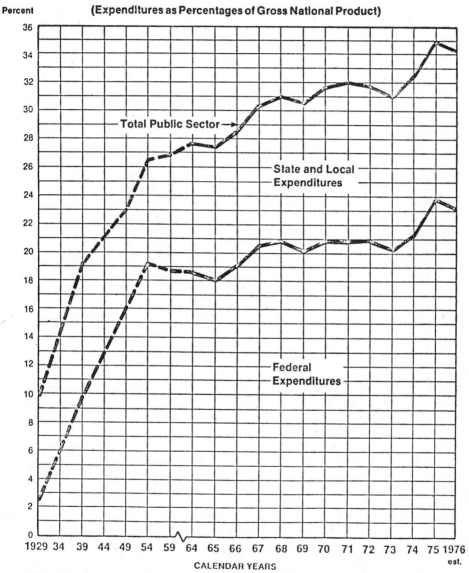

Percent (Expenditures as Percentages of Gross National Product)

Total Public Sector →

State and Local Expenditures

Federal Expenditures

CALENDAR YEARS

Source: Table I.

Significant Features of Fiscal Federalism, Advisory Commission on Inter-governmental Relations, Washington, D.C. (June 1976).

Similarly, in the United States there were two waves of public expenditure increase. The first was a defense shift running from the late 1940s to the mid-1960s. The second was a welfare shift responding to the domestic democratic pressures of the 1960s. (18) This welfare shift resulted in an increase in civilian domestic expenditures from 13.6% of the GNP in 1954 to 26.8% in 1976. About half of this large increase was financed by the combination of new taxes and deficit spending, and the other half by a reallocation of federal expenditures from national defense to welfare-oriented programs. (19)

Decreased Defense Expenditures

It is well established that in most advanced industrial societies welfare expenditures have accounted for a rising share of the budget. Whether defense spending has gone down is less clear and, if it has gone down, whether its decreases are tied to increases in welfare expenditures is even more problematic. Furthermore, even if defense expenditures have decreased, whether this decrease represents a diminished value attached to defense as a national goal is not a settled issue. Morse, developing the tension implicit in his title "Welfare vs. Warfare," demonstrates that in France there is a negative relationship between the two, and his time-series plots as well as verbal arguments bear this out. (20) Nevertheless, I have difficulty accepting this argument as a general proposition for two reasons: one, there is very inconsistent empirical evidence on this question; and two, there are some theoretical reasons for suspecting defense expenditures to move according to their own logic, i.e., according to international pressures.

First, let us turn to the empirical evidence. Bruce Russett, in What Price Vigilance? has examined the trade-offs involved in military expenditures by applying a regression analysis to a large group of countries. His finding for the United States was that "Private consumption has indeed been the largest alternative use of defense money. Guns do come partly at the expense of butter." (21)

However, his general conclusion after studying 120 nations was that there was no correlation between defense spending and public expenditures for health, although he admitted that this aggregate relationship probably masked a negative relationship between defense spending and civilian expenditures in those countries with a high defense budget. (22) Indeed, Russett did find an inverse relationship between military and civilian spending when he carried out the analysis separately on a limited number of countries scoring high on defense expenditures.

The picture is nevertheless still quite murky. Limiting myself to the excellent study by Frederic Pryor, we note that in countries with a high level of defense spending he found a negative relationship between defense and all public civil expenditures with the exception of France, while in other states where the proportion of defense spending in the budget was low he found no relation at all. (23) If any general conclusions can be drawn from all this it is that an inverse relationship exists in political systems with few slack resources, although the troubling paradox with respect to France is still with us.

Empirical data are likely to be highly confusing unless one has all the variables affecting expenditures properly identified and their causal relations similarly well-specified. For this reason the declining military expenditure thesis need not come into question because of its less than universal agreement with the data. The basic idea has a solid theoretical appeal, namely that in a world of finite resources there must be some trade-off between guns and butter. However, there are also some theoretical reasons for supposing that political systems possess a considerable amount of slack resources and that, unless they are operating at the margins (e.g., during war, or in a near complete service state), they will have the flexibility to have both guns and butter. Added to this line of reasoning, we have the argument that many social programs today must be viewed as fixed costs not easily changed by political elites. Social security, unemployment insurance, and health care are viewed as hard-won gains by groups who have struggled for decades to arrive in their present position. This receives indirect support from incremental budgeting theory, where radical reallocations based on altered preferences are further impeded by the ridigifying effect of self-serving program elites who fight to retain their share of the budgeting pie.

The preceding argument concerns the functional relationship between defense spending and welfare expenditures. Now I want to turn to the descriptive consideration of the decline of defense expenditures. I do not think that the levelling off, even the small decline, in defense expenditures in many industrialized countries is necessarily a long-term secular phenomenon. True, there may be a perception of declining usefulness of military force in the contemporary international system, but this is partly linked to transitory factors. In large part it is due to the belief that the backbone of security is found in the mutual vulnerability of all nuclear members of the global system, a doctrine which encourages a ceiling in the arms race beyond which no fruitful political dividend is to be gained by increases in military capability. However, just as the massive retaliation doctrine of the 1950s gave way to the "mutual deterrence based on second-strike capability" of the 1960s, so could deterrence give way to more costly strategies based on defense and damage-limitation capabilities. That this is not a far-fetched idea is indicated by the storm centering around the notorious "Team B" report in the United States today. (24)

In short, the question "How much is enough?" is incomplete; one must add "for what?" If the objective is to preserve second-strike capability or mutual deterrence, there will be definite ceiling effects. This will be so because of the relative ease with which large population centers could be hit using unsophisticated military technologies. To the extent that the nuclear actors pursue counter-value strategies, then little military or political gain will accrue to the side which increases its military hardware. However, if the objectives shift to military targets, a huge increase in expenditure is called for. In this context, the overkill argument becomes less relevant and the critical question becomes one of assuring an adequate survivable deterrent even after absorbing several counter-force exchanges. Here a natural ceiling does not exist as each side must try to match the other's force and still have enough left over to threaten the enemy's population centers.

There is one final point to be made about defense expenditures and defense or military strength as a national goal. There is no necessary relationship between the two. Defense expenditure is only an indicator of the value of defense as a national goal and it is quite possible, even plausible, to argue that this relationship is imperfect or, more accurately, that it is not linear. As former Defense Secretary McNamara admitted, "... a nation can reach a point at which it does not buy more security for itself simply by buying more military hardware... There is a point at which an additional dollar of defense simply no longer buys an additonal dollar's worth of security." (25)

PUBLIC OPINION AND THE NEW NATIONALISM

There are other areas of inquiry where sound empirical investigation would help to uncover answers to our questions. One important area has to do with whether the New Nationalism is anything more than a shift in policy-making preferences or whether it has roots in some more basic public opinion changes. A series of surveys carried out by The Potomac Associates in 1976 indicated that the top ten items of greatest public concern had to do with domestic politics. What's more, the eleventh item was "keeping our military and defense forces strong." (26) This contrasted sharply with a comparable study carried out in 1964 by the Institute for International Social Research which found that the top five items had to do with foreign affairs. This is an important transition to be sure. The difficulty is that we don't know, at least on the limited basis of these data, how permanent these changes are.

According to the concept of the New Nationalism this public opinion shift from foreign to domestic politics, and from defense to welfare objectives, is seen as more than a transitory reversal in priorities; it is a part of a fundamental restructuring of ideas tied to other societal changes. To put the argument in its strongest terms, the major thesis draws from the sociology of Sir Henry Maine, August Comte, and Herbert Spencer which asserts the virtue of industrial society as contrasted to the military basis of feudal societies. As societies evolve toward the industrial, they develop large middle classes who reach their position on the basis of their achievement, and who are more interested in economic advancement than military prowess, duty, or personal honor. (27)

The transition to industrial society involves a triumph of the material over the heroic, the rational-calculating style over the romantic-sentimental, and the pragmatic over the ideological. To put the argument in these explicit terms allows a prior component of the New Nationalism to resurface (the shift from military to economic-welfare goals). Furthermore, this shift is not so new. Ernst Haas had already captured the essence of the essence of the syndrome in an article written in 1963. (28) Speaking of the New Europe, rather than the New Nationalism, the similarities are more striking than the differences.

What are the components of the New Europe? Its main economic component is neither capitalism nor socialism: it is industrialism. Industry, under whatever management, easily produces enough to make everybody comfortable. Minimum standards of consumption are assumed as given for the entire citizenry. If the market mechanism and freely negotiated wage levels fail to attain the minima the state intervenes with subsidies, family allowances, social security payments, educational scholarships and retraining funds..." (29)

To the extent that this argument about the transition to a new society is based on long-term historical force diminishing the war-proneness of industrial societies, it seems incorrect on the basis of the available historical records. Not only have there been lapses into large-scale warfare among industrial societies in the twentieth century, but there has been a progressive militarization of the civilian sector, particularly pronounced in the United States. (30) To be sure, there are constant tensions between the desires for butter and guns but this conflict can't be reduced to psychological correlates, an "economic man" and a "heroic-military man." Still less can they be placed on a historical continuum of societal evolution.

Finally, it is not at all clear that the current era is characterized by a renewed emphasis on the economic values of the industrial era. In fact, writings of Ronald Inglehart offer a challenge to this interpretation. (31) Inglehart is not suggesting for a moment that economic and monetary values are unimportant. Rather, he argues that, precisely because economic goals are so well-secured and we no longer have to struggle to maintain them, we can focus on higher-order goals, such as quality of life, personal growth, and community. Thus, the triumph of post-industrial man is a triumph of the aesthetic-humanistic over the material. If one adopts this perspective, it alters our interpretation of events. While Professor Morse focuses on the 1968 uprisings in France as essentially a worker-consumer reaction against the grosspolitik of deGaulle, others point out the strong romantic, anti-technological component of this "revolution." I suppose Geiger would interpret this event as a romantic, rear-guard reaction against inevitable technological forces.

POLITICAL OPPORTUNITIES AND DANGERS OF THE
NEW NATIONALISM

The evidence presented here is only illustrative, but there is a plausible case that a coherent syndrome of psychological, structural, behavioral, and institutional factors - New Nationalism - is endemic to the historical development of industrial society. If this is true, it suggests a number of political opportunities and dangers which are unequally distributed across different countries.

First of all, there is an opportunity, which according to some is already partially realized, to take advantage of the guns-butter struggle by expanding and then consolidating the pillars of the service state. The time may be ripe for moving ahead in areas such as health, education, social service, transport, and a host of other quality-of-life issues. Though I stick by my earlier argument that the relative decline of military expenditures is partially due to period-specific factors rather than long-term secular processes, it is unlikely that these social gains will be reversed even after pressures for military spending mount.

A second political opportunity flows from the fact that the New Nationalism has developed in a setting where domestic societies are heavily involved in, one might even say "wired into," international and transnational networks of dependence and interdependence. This suggests to me an obvious political response; namely, that states utilize these various contacts as levers of influence to achieve their political goals. Kissinger's explicit mention of linkages in his Pilgrim Speech and the political concessions extracted by Arab states as a result of oil dependence are just two dramatic examples of the manipulation of a structural resource to achieve political goals.

The case for a foreign policy based on interdependence can be made as follows. Interdependencies are made up of a large number of exchanges. Sometimes these exchanges involve goods, at other times services, and at still other times the provision of technology to run an industry. Because of these reciprocal exchanges everyone is vulnerable to the actions of others; the attainment of each one's goals can be upset by the failure of another actor to play his part. Of course, if each actor provided some equally needed commodity to every other actor there might be a stalemate of capabilities at this level too, but such equality in the distribution of dependencies does not exist. The global picture instead suggests great inequalities or asymmetries in the ties among nations, and it is these asymmetries which could be exploited for foreign-policy objectives. Indeed, this argument becomes all the more attractive in the context of the discussion on the declining utility of military force. Exchange asymmetries have obvious attractions in contrast to military force. Economic power rests on resources which are homogenous and fungible while military power rests on resources that are heterogenous and lumpy. Thus one of the primary problems in the utilization of military power is to match the weapon with the political objective. Since economic power rests on an infinitely divisible resource base, money, no such problems are encountered in its use.

There have already been several suggestions for the United States to follow a strategy of interdependence. (32) Indeed, the term "interdependence" has filled the policy journals (e.g., Department of State Bulletin) just as it has the academic sources. The implications of this transition, from military to economic instruments of foreign policy, are very important and unsettling. Within a global context, the advanced, capitalist societies would almost surely be advantaged, since they are the ones with the most extensive international networks. Within the Atlantic context, the United States would be the big winner and, indeed, it may be argued that the United States has been playing its economic cards for a long time.

There are some real dangers in the New Nationalism also. If the battlefield shifts from warheads, planes, and tanks to trade policy, technology transfer, and capital flows, if the key form of agreement shifts from treaty to contract, the smaller and poorer countries will probably be even more disadvantaged than previously. Small states which were able to exert disproportionate influence because of their strategic location, or simply because they were a valuable ally or neutral in the event of war, may find themselves without any trump cards. It is perhaps understandable that a renewed interest in strategies of self-reliance, individual and collective, is taking place at the same time that international politics is taking on a new focus.

There are other political dangers in the New Nationalism. E.H. Carr saw in the triad of service state, nationalization of economic policy, and geographic extension of nationalism the "characteristic totalitarian symptoms" of our times. (33) Without attempting to shed any light on that question, we should observe that modern industrial society does have a pathological aspect; in fact, there is a whole syndrome of "diseases" associated with it: the overloading of governments, the emergence of sub-national ethnicity, the decline in party identification, the "stalled society," the increasing demands on the part of the interest groups for a larger, guaranteed portion of the pie, the "democratic distemper," the depletion of "slack" resources, and other factors have worked to produce increasing problems in the governability of advanced industrial societies.

INTELLECTUAL OPPORTUNITIES AND DANGERS

Political opportunities and dangers are mirrored in the academic world. If what we call the New Nationalism comes to dominate the present period, we will have an unprecedented opportunity to build links, perhaps to merge more closely the fields of economics and political science, a division that to some has always been frustrating. Oddly enough, the difficulty caused by the split between these two disciplines was brought about by the same forces giving rise to the New Nationalism, in particular by a trend toward specialization. This reintegration will be aided by the fact that economic policy is becoming increasingly politicized and the fact that it is becoming correspondingly more difficult to understand political or economic phenomena in isolation from one another. The distinction between high and low politics will become less useful as an analytical tool becauase it will correspond less and less to the political economy of international politics.

Another intellectual opportunity provided by the New Nationalism centers on the closer integration of domestic and international politics. International politics will be seen to operate less and less according to its "own logic," if by that we mean a set of rules dictated only by the interactions of states. The old maxim "Politics stops at the water's edge" will be soundly rejected in favor of a growing trend toward the domestication of international politics, a trend reflecting the incorporation of many interest groups into the process of foreign policy-making. In addition, the expanded role of government, especially in social-welfare areas, will encourage governments to control and manage the domestic consequences of events in the international system. To the question of whether the New Nationalism is inward-looking or outward-looking, I would reply that it is inward with respect to goals, and outward with respect to means. There is no contradiction here.

There are also some real intellectual dangers and dead ends posed by the concept of New Nationalism, and we would do well to consider them squarely from the outset. The first pitfall is the danger of the New Nationalism becoming just another "new" which, along with a variety of "posts" and "neos," is relegated to the wastebasket of discarded concepts. We should remind ourselves that a spate of articles on the New Nationalism were written in the early 1950s, (34) yet hardly anyone can recall what these authors meant by the use of the term. To return to the main line of argument, I sense a disturbing tendency to form new categories out of mere descriptive differences in an essentially uni-dimensional variable, to elevate differences in intensity to qualitative differences so that a resurgency of nationalism becomes the New Nationalism rather than a greater magnitude of some well-known nationalism. The question whether the phenomena identified by the term New Nationalism are new in any qualitative sense is open. To my knowledge, very little serious empirical work has been done in the area of empirical typologies of nationalism.

In the absence of strong evidence of the qualitative distinctiveness of the New Nationalism, my preference is to treat this phenomenon in a historically continuous manner. To jump to premature conclusions about creating new categories runs two serious risks for the academic community. First, it works against the cumulation and integration of our research and understanding. Since different scholars see themselves as working on different problems, they will not be encouraged to either draw or add to a continuous body of knowledge. Rather each scholarly community will approach its task de novo and fashion it out of whole cloth. In like manner, we will not be prompted to search for historical parallels of the same underlying phenomena and to see different forms as expressions of more basic historically continuous regularities.

The last third of the nineteenth century ushered in an expansive period labelled the New Imperialism and was characterized by the politicization of international economic relations. According to E. H. Carr, the infusion of statist control into economic transactions during this period parallels the increasing political content of economic relations during the post-war period. (35) For our purposes here, it is important to note that the nineteenth century transition at the international level was linked to important domestic changes, both at the level of classes and regimes, suggesting as a hypothesis similarly important domestic changes today.

A second danger, centering around the ideological implications of the New Nationalism, results from two somewhat contradictory tendencies. The first tendency is to view the New Nationalism as inward-looking and defensive in nature. Hence the nation-state will cease to be troublesome simply because it is less concerned with the affairs of others. The second tendency receives support from the rhetoric of interdependence, a view which suggests a world where everyone's fate is tied up with the well-being of others. In both interpretations, nationalism is interpreted in a benign light, though for different reasons. I believe both of these interpretations misunderstand the nature of the beast. The first view confuses isolationism with nationalism. To become more nationalistic does not necessarily mean to turn inward. The psychological profile given by The Potomac Associates is very definitely one of nationalism - not isolationism. (36) National groups will still operate in an external environment, though for their own private economic goals. There will be less open-ended support for the United Nations and for allies. The second view confuses dependence with interdependence, a confusion increased by the pursual of Project Independence by the United States during the same period in which interdependence occupies an important verbal positon in policy statements. Though the rhetoric of interdependence conjures up images of "spaceship Earth" and "joint fate," in reality a policy of interdependence can have a more self-serving side, flowing from a recognition of the large asymmetries in international relations. (37) We would be remiss as scholars if we did not attempt to expose the concrete interest basis of interdependence.

My final fear is that the nation-state will not be the most helpful level of analysis to understand many of the important changes we have described. As E. H. Carr has shown, (38) there have been many prior historic changes in foreign economic policy and these have usually been accompanied by important domestic realignments of classes or interest groups and of the linkages between these groups and central political institutions. If the concept of New Nationalism encourages us to look within the nation at the separate domestic forces, it will be much more productive than a focus on the nation as an abstract, undifferentiated entity. Whom does the New Nationalism and interdependence benefit? Why are textile and steel industries in the U.S. protectionist while high technology industries and agriculture are internationalists? What combination of societal-governmental forces are served by fostering this particular mix of attitudinal withdrawal and behavioral interdependence? Which groups are served by a protectionist stance and which by an interdependent posture? A large agenda of researchable topics lies ahead.

NOTES

(1) Henry Kissinger, "Toward a Global Community." Speech before the Indian Council on World Affairs, New Delhi, October 28, 1973, Department of State, Press Release 445, p. 5.

(2) The term New Nationalism has been used and discussed by several scholars: Theodore Geiger, The Fortunes of the West: The Future of Atlantic Relations (Bloomington, Indiana: University of Indiana Press, 1973); Geiger, "A New U.S. Hegemony in Western Europe?" Looking Ahead, Vol. 22, No. 1 (February 1974), pp. 1-8; and Edward L. Morse, Modernization and the Transformation of International Relations (New York, NY: Free Press, 1976).

(3) Hans Kohn, Nationalism: Its Meaning and History (Princeton, New Jersey: D. Van Nostrand Co., Inc., revised edition, 1965).

(4) Karl W. Deutsch, Nationalism and Its Alternatives (New York: Alfred A. Knopf, 1969), p. 14.

(5) Geiger, Fortunes of the West, p. 51.

(6) Ibid., p. 52.

(7) Geiger, "A New U.S. Hegemony in Western Europe?", p. 2.

(8) For a study dealing with the psychological syndrome of modernism: Alex Inkeles and David H. Smith, Becoming Modern (Cambridge, Mass.: Harvard University Press, 1974). For extensive treatments of the post-industrial syndrome: Ronald Ingelhart, The Silent Revolution: Changing Values and Political Style Among Western Publics (Princeton, New Jersey: Princeton University Press, 1977); and Ronald Inglehart, "The Nature of Value Change in Post-Industrial Societies," in Leon N. Lindberg (ed.) Politics and the Future of Industrial Society (New York: David McKay Co., 1976), pp. 57-99.

(9) Morse, Modernization and the Transformation of International Relations, pp. 19-20.

(10) Bruce M. Russett, What Price Vigilance? (New Haven, Conn.: Yale University Press, 1970), Ch. 5.

(11) Harold B. Malmgren, "Managing Foreign Economic Policy," Foreign Policy, No. 6 (Spring 1972), p. 43.

(12) For descriptive information on the growth of this international role I am relying heavily on Raymond F. Hopkins, "The International Role of 'Domestic' Bureaucracy," International Organization, Vol. 30, No. 3 (Summer 1976).

(13) Geiger, Fortunes of the West, p. 51.

(14) Deutsch, Nationalism and Its Alternatives, p. 28.

(15) Ibid.

(16) Significant Features of Fiscal Federalism (Washington, D.C.: Advisory Commission on Intergovernmental Relations, 1976), p. 1.

(17) Edward L. Morse, "Defense Autonomy in Gaullist France: Welfare versus Warfare and the Dilemma of Insufficient Resources," (Morristown, New Jersey: General Learning Press, 1972), pp. 4-10.

(18) Samuel P. Huntington, "The Democratic Distemper," The Public Interest, No. 41 (Fall 1975), p. 13.

(19) Significant Aspects of Fiscal Federalism, Advisory Commission on Intergovernmental Relations (Washington, D.C.: June 1976), p. 1.

(20) Such a conclusion can be inferred from a juxtaposition of Figures 1 and 2 along with supplementary data presented in the text.

(21) Russett, What Price Vigilance? P. 141.

(22) Ibid, p. 159.

(23) Frederic Pryor, Public Expenditures in Communist and Capitalist Nations (Homewood, Illinois: Irwin, 1969), pp. 120-121 and 124. Cited in Russett, What Price Vigilance?

(24) For the thinking of this team, see Richard Pipes, "Why the Soviet Union Thinks It Could Fight and Win a Nuclear War," Commentary, Vol. 64, No. 1 (July 1977).

(25) Robert S. McNamara, "Accelerating Population Stabilization through Social and Economic Progress," Overseas Development Council, Development Paper 24 (Washington, D.C., 1977), p. 1

(26) William Watts and Lloyd A. Free, "Nationalism, Not Isolationism," Foreign Policy, No. 24 (Fall 1976), p. 10.

(27) See "introduction" to Part III of WAR, "War, Liberal Democracy and Industrial Society," Leon Bramson and George W. Goethals, revised edition (New York: Basic Books, Inc., 1968), pp. 295-298 and Herbert Spencer, "The Military and the Industrial Society," same source, pp. 299-316.

(28) Ernst B. Haas, "Technocracy, Pluralism, and the New Europe," in Stephen R. Graubard (ed.) A New Europe? (Boston, Mass.: Houghton, Mifflin and Co., 1964), pp. 62-88.

(29) Haas, "Technocracy, Pluralism, and the New Europe," p. 68.

(30) Adam Yarmolinsky, The Military Establishment (New York: Harper and Row, 1971).

(31) The most recent, and certainly most comprehensive, statement by Inglehart is contained in The Silent Revolution: Changing Values and Political Styles Among Western Publics (Princeton, N.J.: Princeton University Press, 1977).

(32) See, for example, Malcolm W. Hoag, "United States Foreign Policy: Why Not Project Interdependence by Design?" (Los Angeles, California: International Institute for Economic Research, Reprint Paper 2, October 1976), pp. 1-30; and Robert H. Johnson, "Managing Interdependence: Restructuring the U.S. Government," Overseas Development Council, Development Paper 23 (Washington, D.C., Overseas Development Council, 1977), pp. 1-23.

(33) E.H. Carr, Nationalism and After (London: MacMillan and Co., Ltd., 1945), p. 26.

(34) For example, Walter Sulzbach, "The New Nationalism," South Atlantic Quarterly LI (October 1952) and William G. Carleton, "The New Nationalism," Virginia Quarterly Review (July, 1950).

(35) Carr, Nationalism and After, p. 18.

(36) Watts and Free, "Nationalism, Not Isolationism."

(37) For a critique of the "rhetoric of interdependence," see Denis Goulet, "World Interdependence: Verbal Smokescreen or New Ethic?" Development Paper 21 (Washington, D.C.: Overseas Development Council, 1976), pp. 1-32.

(38) Carr, Nationalism and After.

The New Nationalism
and External Policies

3 The Nation-State and the Coordination of Foreign Policies
F.S. Northedge

NATION-STATES AND THE INTERNATIONAL SYSTEM

The subject of this paper is the contemporary nation-state, the basic unit of our present world political system, and the problem of coordinating the foreign policies, or mutual relations, of these 150 or so entities which now divide the globe among them. Our starting point is that the human race is at present distributed among these territorial and legal associations, the states, which provide the most important frameworks of our lives and constitute the chief foci of our daily loyalties; that each of these states is sovereign in the sense that its executive body, the government, is the supreme source of law within its territory, unless the state's constitution declares otherwise, and that, in its external relations, it cannot be bound by the law of the international system (with some exceptions) without its consent; and finally, that these states are nation-states in the sense that their territorial limits tend to coincide with the boundaries of national sentiment, and that the justification of government, since at least the French Revolution of 1789, has come increasingly to be regarded as the advancement of the interests of that group whose members think of themselves as a nation.

While the above description of the international system may be accepted in general terms, there are at least three qualifications which some may wish to make. The first is that the nation-state as it existed prior to 1939 is rapidly ceasing to be the only, or even the dominant, unit of international relations. Men and women the world over increasingly regard themselves as linked together across the old national boundaries in innumerable associations - social, cultural, economic, professional, as well as political - and are consequently less and less conscious of the fact that they are French, German, Italian, and so on, and more and more conscious of their common interests as teachers, engineers, airline pilots, or deep-sea divers of the world. The second qualification is that the nation-state which prior to 1939 was conceived as a monolith of "billiard-ball" hardness, is now penetrated by a million or more trans-national threads which tie its people to others like themselves in similarly penetrated states. The states of the world, it is argued, are in fact being phased out as modern world-wide science and technology spread their networks over increasingly outdated frontiers. (1) The third qualification to our original picture of a world system of independent states is that the quality of national feeling behind political frontiers has been in the process of change over the past twenty years or so. People today look to their government less for the achievement of traditional objectives (military glory, empire, national honor, and defense of the homeland) and rather more for prosaic and material satisfactions (jobs, stable currencies, equilibria in the balance of payments, the conservation of national resources, and protection of the environment). This change in the quality of national feeling is no doubt implied in the expression the New Nationalism, which has been adopted as the central theme of the present Conference.

t   We need not dwell on the first two qualifications mentioned above. It is sufficient to say, in regard to the first, that the demise of the nation-state has been announced more than once by writers since World War II, but, like the death of Mark Twain which he saw reported in a newspaper, it has time and again proved premature. (2) The fact that in these last thirty years the creation of new nation-states has been proceeding at a break-neck speed with the unfolding of decolonization; that few, if any, of these new states, or indeed of the old states, show much willingness to surrender their independence in multi-national federations; that modern national governments seem to exercise, if anything, an increasing control over their people's lives, and certainly to spend more and more of the nation's income - all this seems to show that the nation-state remains a tough and lively animal, even though other creatures may have joined it in recent years as members of the international zoo. As to the second qualification, arising from the alleged penetration of modern states by international forces such as commerce, propaganda, and subversion, certainly this has been and remains a fact of current history. At the same time, the modern state has developed its own antidotes to penetration by external influences. An internationalist, for example, who sought to correct the nationalistic biases in the schools and universities of today, especially in the newer countries of Africa and Asia, would probably find that he had let himself in for an uphill, if not positively dangerous, task. It is impossible to be overly precise about these two issues, or qualifications as we have called them, of the nation-state, but we should be careful not to write off too soon that body as the basic unit of the international system.

The third qualification to our basic premise is that national feelings and the demands made on national governments by their constituents have changed, and are continuing to change. National policies in a world where human life and social institutions are at all times in flux, are increasingly concerned with economic and social security. The governments of the world today, as the United Nations Charter declares, are committed to social and economic objectives leading to the betterment of their people's lives in a material sense. This takes precedence over the traditional objectives of the rulers of states. (3) These social and economic concerns have virtually become a condition of government in the fourth quarter of the twentieth century, and the rest of this paper will be concerned with the impact of this change in the function of government on the foreign policies of states and the problem of coordinating those policies.

At the same time, it is important to insist that this New Nationalism is much older than many of those who have written about it seem to think. It is modern socialism, total war, and the Great Depression of the early 1930s which must be regarded as the triple progenitors of the social dimension now evident in modern foreign policy. These shook the old-style, free-for-all capitalism to its foundations and created the contemporary dirigisme de l'état. The effects can be seen dramatically if we compare the social and economic content of the United Nations Charter of 1945, with the old-world League of Nations Covenant of 1919, though even that aspect of the Charter has to be considered against the background of the Bruce Committee Report of 1939. This Committee proposed the creation within the League framework of a group similar to the present United Nations Economic and Social Council, an effect, again, of the impact of the world economic turbulence of the 1930s on thinking about international organization. (4) We must assume, too, that the current detente in East-West relations has had some effect, which may regretfully be transient, in making the economic and social content of foreign policy seem more attractive to public opinion in the Western democracies than the old political and security considerations. However that may be, our first task must be to examine the sort of effects the New Nationalism has had on modern foreign policies and the problems of their coordination.

FOREIGN POLICIES

Two such effects are worthy of notice. One is that, while there has been throughout the entire history of the international system an interplay among the internal and external policies of the different states, that feature has perhaps never been so marked as it is today. Accordingly a scholarly theory - the "linkage theory" - has been devised, perhaps superfluously, to explain and describe it. (5) It is not merely that, as of old, ministers in deliberating their foreign policies have to take into account continuously the likely effect of their decisions on the internal support they and their political parties enjoy; nor is it that many more ministers and departments of state are implicated in the making of foreign policy today than were in 1939. (6) The fact is that the present-day diplomat is continuously dealing in foreign capitals with matters as widely remote from his traditional concerns as the ingredients in ice cream or the structure of the nets used by fishermen in his home state. The dividing line between home affairs and foreign affairs still exists, but it has become so frayed as to be at some points scarcely visible at all.

The second effect of the New Nationalism is to make more difficult, perhaps impossible, the exact definition of foreign policy, whether of a nation-state or any other entity. What precisely is a foreign policy which the executive of a state is supposed to decide on the advice of his professional civil servants, his diplomatic service, his armed forces, and his other agents who implement policy outside the state's frontiers? In particular, how, in the age of the New Nationalism, are foreign policies to be distinguished from economic policies? Economic policies, internal and external, are today surely so inextricably blended with the whole conduct of one state's relations with its international partners that the effort to single out the coordination of foreign policies must seem artificial at best and utterly impossible at worst. Is there such a unique thing as foreign policy, and, if so, what is it?

We need not worry too much about the difficulty of achieving mathematical exactitude in demarcating the province of foreign policy as a responsibility of governments, and in stating the points at which it may be differentiated from their other responsibilities. In broad terms, it would seem that the foreign policy, or the political aspects of foreign relations, involves three sorts of dealings between one country and another. First, there is a reference to the general, or overall, official attitudes of one state to another, or to the international community as a whole. Such attitudes will generally consist of a myriad of positions on more or less specialized questions such as defense, or commercial, monetary, cultural, ideological, legal, and social relations; nevertheless, a Foreign Minister will know what he means, and others will generally know what he means, when he says, "Our relations with country X are at the moment cordial," or "cool," or whatever epithet he may use. It is usually against the background of that general state of relations that relations on particular questions will be considered and determined.

Secondly, when we use the word politics - assuming that by foreign policy we are referring more to the political dimension of international relations - we tend to have in mind matters of status, standing, power, position in some sort of hierarchy, and of relationships of deference, authority, and subordination. Whether the drive for power is or is not the dominating motive behind state behavior in the system of states, it is a matter of common observation that no state can be indifferent to the distribution of power, or to its ability to shape events in the international system. Each state must question whether that distribution is relatively favorable or unfavorable to its own purposes.

Thirdly, we should expect foreign policy and indeed all political activity, of which foreign policy is no more or less than a branch, to be concerned with the advancement, and certainly with the defense, of the general social and political values in which the state and its people profess to believe. What sort of world do they want to see and live in? What would they like to see happen at home and abroad? What would they regard as disasters? How would they muster their best efforts, with perhaps their lives at stake, to avert calamity? How important to them is it that they be governed in a certain way, and what sort of price would they be prepared to pay to make doubly sure that they were not governed in another way? These are some of the questions that a country's foreign policy tries to answer. We must remember that these are not academic questions, raised and debated merely for the sake of argument, but are related to the most inward and powerful springs of action of a nation, while at the same time they are intertwined with all its material interests as the nation and its leaders see them.

Foreign policy, then, may be described as concerned with the general conduct of business with other states. It strives for a balance of world or regional forces which is favorable as far as possible to the state's own interests and purposes, however conceived; and its object is the maintenance and strengthening of the kind of political and social order at home and abroad in which the state, or the most influential fraction of its people, actually believe. As such, we must take note of the obvious point that foreign policy (despite its name) is much less the execution of a premeditated plan of action, even for the most powerful states, than are most domestic policies. Since the implementation of foreign policy, for practically all states at practically all times, is the unending attempt to secure the cooperation of other states in the fulfillment of one's own purpose, and since in the last resort it is for those other states to determine whether they will cooperate, and on what terms, the Foreign Minister needs to be an opportunist who attends upon events and seizes the right moment and the right conjuncture of affairs.

He plays a different role than the reformer who guides a bill to change land tenure or a law of conveyancing through all its stages in the legislature.

This brings us to a second major point about foreign policy: the close relation that exists between foreign and economic policy, and between a country's foreign policy, as we have defined it, and its economic position and interests. This relation is a complicated one. First, we must revert to the point made earlier that foreign policy is usually thought of as embracing the general relations of one state with another, and that the economic relations of states - trade, lending and borrowing, the process of investment, the ownership and control of resources, and the movement of labor from one country to another - will generally be regarded as a section or branch of those general relations. Normally, the Foreign Minister and the Foreign Office will have a great deal to do with and perhaps have the final word in such economic questions, unless there is some good reason to the contrary, such as traditional usage or the standing or authority of other Ministers. As a rule, one can expect a certain amount of tension to exist between Foreign Office attitudes to internal economic questions and the attitudes of other ministries, such as those dealing with finance or foreign trade which are most specialized in such questions. A Foreign Office may be inclined, for instance, to see wider implications in the sale of arms to another country than the department concerned with overseas trade. Its dispositon will be, where such differences arise with other departments of state, to maintain the general, overall view and try to ensure that pressures of an economic kind which develop within the country do not jeopardize the broad balance of national interests which foreign policy seeks to promote.

There are more particular ways in which a country's economic position and interests will affect its foreign policy. There is the obvious relationship between the strength and stability of the country's economic base and the kind of commitments the country can afford to assume in the international field and the effectiveness with which it can discharge them. The bearing of economic strength on the scale of foreign policy commitments and the effectiveness of foreign policy is not, of course, always direct; Britain's political influence in the world is still no doubt greater than Japan's despite the disparity in economic strength between the two.   Nevertheless, the generalization remains valid notwithstanding exceptions.

Secondly, one should expect that the balance of economic strength between the different sections of opinions within a country have some effect on the conduct of its foreign relations and the kind of priorities in foreign policy that are determined by its government. The strength of French farming interests and fishing interests of Britain, for example, has had important implications not only for France's and Britain's trading partners abroad, but for their political associates in the international system as well.

Thirdly, the economic interests of a country as a whole, meaning the kind of economic conditions at home and abroad which the people of that country, or important groups within it, consider valuable to themselves, are high on the list of the things which the government must strive to defend and advance in its dealings with other states. By looking at what a nation, or the politically important parts of it, considers economically beneficial to itself, we can form clues as to why that nation has the sort of foreign policy it has. It may be, and indeed it would be surprising if this were not the case, that these economic interests are, for a particular state at a particular time, partially or wholly in conflict with the other external interests of the state, whether these be political, strategic, ideological, or whatever. In that case, and if the conflict is serious enough to warrant consideration at the highest level, the issue may be resolved by ministers, including the Foreign Minister, working together. We may be sure that if this sort of consideration were given to the issue it would be treated as a foreign policy matter and dealt with within the overall framework of the country's foreign policy. This is another way of saying that if the economic interests were allowed to take precedence over non-economic interests, that would not be a decision of economic policy but of foreign policy, and it would have to be correlated with the country's general foreign policy line.

THE COORDINATION OF FOREIGN POLICIES

When we now consider the coordination of the foreign policies of the various nation-states, it is evident this problem has two aspects, the internal and the external. The internal aspect has, in its turn, two sides: one is that of introducing some sort of order or equilibrium into the different domestic pressures and interests which are focused in any country on the foreign policy-making agencies; the other is that of reconciling and relating to each other government's domestic policies - those concerned with the internal administration of the country - and its foreign policy.

The task of balancing the different demands which emerge within a country for pursuing one course or another (or refraining from so doing) in the field of external policy, is essentially that of the government of the day. Ministers, conscious of the likely effect of their decisions on their standing in the country, must make up their minds which pressure group is going to have how much of its demands reflected in the position the government takes on the different issues as they flow through the international system. In arriving at a consensus on this matter, the various ministers are bound to vary in the influence they exert; it may not always be the Foreign Minister, or even the head of the government, who has the major say. Nevertheless, the Cabinet or chief executive, if the matter is one of sufficiently high politics to be debated at that level, will in effect be making the foreign policy of the country in the sense of determining the priorities to be accorded to the different internal demands pressing for expression in the government's international policy. At the same time, as well as being a channel through which internal demands are mediated to the internal system, the foreign policy makers will try to project into the country's external relations some conception of what they themselves think the general national interest demands.

There is the second internal problem of coordination, that of reconciling the various domestic policies the government is pursuing with the matters it is seeking to promote in its international relations. Care has to be taken, for instance, to ensure that a policy for combating unemployment in a country goes hand-in-hand with efforts to encourage the country's trading partners abroad to maintain a high rate of economic growth. Efforts to conserve oil by restricting the fuel consumption of motor cars may damage the car-exporting interests of an allied state. The coordination of internal and external policies is necessary to minimize the risks of this happening. One way in which this sort of coordination is practiced today is, as we have seen, by introducing into the diplomatic system many departments of state other than the Foreign Ministry, and by expanding the diplomatic mission abroad to include officials from home departments dealing with such matters as finance, trade, industry, science, and education. Another expedient, favored by the British Central Policy Review Staff in its "Report on Overseas Representation," published in August, 1977, is the breaking down of barriers between the Foreign Service and home civil service departments and the ending of the exclusivity of the diplomatic career. (7) The current economic difficulties of the industrialized non-communist states, especially Britain, may have led some of their people to think of foreign policy as little but the promotion of internal economic needs. In a world as crowded and interdependent as ours the importance of coordination in the sense described here hardly needs emphasis.

But it is coordination in the external sense, the harmonization of the foreign policy of one country with that of another and of the foreign policy of all countries together, so far as may be possible, that concerns us more. This is indeed the classic and permanent problem of international relations, though, as we will see, the New Nationalism has given an extra dimension to it. It is for coordination in this classical and external sense that diplomacy and the whole machinery of internal relations, from the permanent mission in the foreign capital to the huge, bureaucratic international organization of the United Nations, exist.

The need for the coordination, or perhaps we should say the attempted coordination, of foreign policies in this sense arises from two bedrock realities of international relations: the fact that the power of all states, meaning their capacity to produce the effects they intend, is limited; and the fact that, although that universal limitation exists, the presumption neverthe-less is that each and every state is sovereign and has the right to say "No" to any proposal set in front of it.

That the power of all states is limited hardly needs demonstration. Even the greatest super-power cannot, merely by saying so, get the rest of the world to move in the way it wants and at the speed it wants. Every state is seeking the cooperation of other states on terms favorable to itself as far as possible whether the issue under discussion is a matter of freedom of movement in occupied Berlin or the classification of eggs in the European Common Market. People sometimes distinguish between praiseworthy states which are cooperative and states which say "Nyet" or "No," and slam the door behind them. However, there is not a single state in the world which will not cooperate with other states, provided that the terms of cooperation are favorable to it. Indeed, the different states have no other option but to cooperate since, as we have said, even the greatest powers can hardly do anything for themselves on their own. A state or government which really hopes to "go it alone" in international affairs, and which refuses to make the effort to coordinate its foreign policy with the policies of other states, is ignoring the most fundamental realities of the international system and doing its interests no good in the bargain.

We have insisted that a state must try to coordinate its policies with its neighbors on its own terms, or rather on as much of its own terms as it can; and a situation can, of course, arise in which the prospective terms of coordination seem likely to be so unfavorable that it is wiser to call off the attempt at coordination, at least for the time being. The reason for this is the obvious one, which we have already mentioned, namely that all states have the right in the last analysis to cooperate with other states on certain determinate terms. They have that right under the law of the international system, unless that right is otherwise legally restricted, and they have the right in practice. Since 1945 it has proved exceedingly difficult for any one state, even a great power, to compel another state, even a small country, to do something or refrain from doing something, except in the rather unusual case where the second state was wholly within the military grip of the first state. In a normal situation a country uses its efforts to get the most favorable terms it can, with the option of breaking off the transaction and trying again later if acceptable terms are not to be had, and if the prospects are not likely to get even worse in the meantime.

But how does this universal process of coordination, or attempted coordination, proceed? What in effect it amounts to is that a formula has to be worked out which in some way represents the conceived interests of the two sides where the attempted coordination is bilateral, or of all sides where it is multilateral. The terms of accommodation must be such that it seems better on balance to the two or more sides to accept them rather than to try to secure more favorable terms by the use of force, or by breaking off the transaction temporarily or permanently. In this process of mutual adjustment the two or more sides will mobilize behind their arguments all the inducements in their power, ranging from more or less persuasive advocacy to more or less veiled threats of the consequences for the other side or sides if a settlement on the indicated terms is not reached. The purpose of this mobilization of blandishment and threats by each side or every side is to heighten the interest of the other, or others, in a settlement on the proffered conditions and at the same time to enhance the costs and drawbacks of not reaching a settlement. Obviously, the more extensive and varied the spectrum of threats and promises which a state's representatives can take into the negotiating process, the more likely are they to realize the state's objectives on acceptable terms.

The coordination of foreign policies is therefore a primary and essential function of the international system. If the world were governed from a single center, the coordination of policies would be unnecsssary, or would take on a radically different form: there would be one policy determined by the central authority and issued as fiat to the peripheral units, though some bargaining might still be needed to secure the implementation of such centrally promulgated directives. In another situation, the coordination of their policies on issues great and small with one another depends on how far their interests are identical or convergent. This has always been the rule, with historical variations, in the international system. There is no good reason why it should not continue to be the rule as long as the structure of the international system remains roughly as it is. But, as we have emphasized, nation-states have changed and are changing, and one of these changes is what we call the New Nationalism.

THE NEW NATIONALISM AND THE COORDINATION OF FOREIGN POLICIES

The question we must now consider is whether, on balance, the New Nationalism, meaning the shift since 1945 in the order of priority from the political and strategic aims of modern governments in their external policies to predominantly economic and social aims - if indeed there has been such a shift - has made the coordination of external policies between the different states relatively easier or harder. Do the states of the world today find that they have more or less difficulty than they did before the age of socialization of foreign policy in integrating their external relations or simply in getting on with one another? The modern government is heavily preoccupied with economic commitments, with maintaining full employment, with achieving a healthy economic growth, with monetary stability, and with the conservation and economic use of resources. Is this preoccupation a factor making for international cooperation, good neighborliness, and the integration of states and their policies, or does it foster divisiveness, national exclusiveness and competition?

Here we are presented with a paradox: that is, the apparent contradiction between what may be called the tendency of interested and learned opinion on these questions and the evidence of the senses. On the one hand, since approximately 1918, there has been a distinct trend in the thinking of liberals and social democrats in Western countries, and certainly in Anglo-Saxon countries, to regard political nationalism as retrograde, divisive, and a positive danger to world peace. Furthermore, it has been conceived as giving way to more civilized forms of world society as a sense of the economic interdependence of the modern world makes itself felt. The conflict of "political myths" and "economic realities," it was thought in circles sympathetic to the League of Nations in the 1920s, must surely be resolved with the ultimate victory of a world-wide community tightly, though insensibly, bound together by commerce and industry. (8) The economic depression of the early 1930s and the totalitarian nationalism which sprang out of it were severe setbacks to this easy-going internationalism. However, a new impulse was given to it as World War II drew to its close. This was reflected in the thinking on post-war reconstruction represented, again mainly in the West, by the Atlantic Charter of August, 1941 and the Bretton Woods agreements of 1944. The East-West Cold War, coming so shortly after the defeat of the Axis Powers, was a further setback. However, no sooner did a thaw appear in the democratic states' relations with Moscow in the 1960s than writers on international relations in the West, especially in the United States, began to affirm once more that, through developments like the mushrooming of international non-governmental organizations and the growth of a common interest in safeguarding the global environment, the old political divisions of the human race were losing their relevance. "Toward a Politics of the Planet Earth" was one of the slogans of the new creed. (9)

Yet these prognostications of a new world social order, with its foundations in present-day economic and technological interdependence, seems to be belied by the actual practices of the different national communities in the world today.   If the volume of international trade and investment, the temporary and permanent movement of people from one spot on the earth's surface to another, the number of letters, cables, telephone calls, parcels, passing from one country to another are all on the increase from one year to another, this mobility does not yet seem to be reflected in much actual constitutional amalgamation of the different states. People may, with every appearance of conviction, reiterate the shibboleth that the world "must federate or perish," but many indeed seem as though they would rather perish than federate. Perhaps the supreme evidence of the contradiction today between the fact of economic interdependence and the persistence of nationalism is the circumstance that even in western Europe, which has drunk to the dregs the bitter cup of nationalism, the integration of states proceeds at a pitifully slow pace, if indeed there is any perceptible movement at all. In Eastern Europe, where the Soviet writ runs, such integration as has been effected in bodies such as Comecon seems to be regarded by most people there as a form of incarceration from which they would gladly escape if they could. In most of the rest of the world, there seems to be little in the way of a visible move to commit national suicide in order to be reborn again in some federal complex. Indeed, in many parts of the world today it is not the unification of national states that is the remarkable thing, but its opposite: the tendency of sub-groups and minor nationalities either to break away from larger units and form states of their own or to demand some appreciable installment of autonomy within their existing states.

How may this paradox - the consensus, or seeming consensus, of "informed" opinion, or influential sections of it, as against daily evidence of the senses - be reconciled, especially in the light of current interest in what we have called the New Nationalism? One answer is that the logic of the economic system of the modern developed national states does indeed call for international cooperation and the coordination of national policies on a scale and to a degree of intimacy never before experienced in history; but that, simply because the nations are brought together by the sort of economic needs which they have today, their fundamental differences of interest become even more blatant. To resort to an analogy from another sphere, the problems which husbands and wives face through their continuous and intimate cohabitation are infinitely more perplexing than those of casual acquaintances who meet only briefly from time to time. Interdependence, in other words, can be a source of conflict as much as a program of mutual support.

The truth of this is evident if we examine some of the effects of economic wants and interests on the relations between states. The familiar distinction between the developed and the developing countries - the North and South of the world - is a useful point at which to begin since it strikingly illustrates the symbiotic relationship we have in mind between international interdependence and the international conflict of policies. The North-South dialogue amply illustrates the fact that nations may need each other for the satisfaction of their economic requirements, but that is no assurance that they will be able to coordinate their policies.

The developing countries, symbolized by the original "Group of 77" which dominated UNCTAD (the United Nations Conference on Trade and Development) since its first meeting in Geneva in 1964, have sought to improve the terms of their trade with the developed industrialized countries. This campaign has now taken on the struggle in the name of the New International Economic Order (NIEO). (10) Encouraged by the extraordinary success of the oil-producing countries in OPEC (Organization of Petroleum Exporting Countries) in raising oil prices some five-fold since 1973, other raw-material-producing states have striven to improve their bargaining power vis-a-vis the consumer countries by a variety of devices oriented chiefly toward the stabilizing and, in appropriate cases, the raising of commodity prices. The effects have been at one and the same time to strengthen international cooperation and to widen even further the differences between states. On the one hand, the oil-rich states undoubtedly owe their price victory, and their present abounding wealth, to the solidarity and strength of OPEC. This is reflected in the recognition by the UNCTAD-77 group as a whole that in solidarity must lie their chief hopes of success. On the other hand, the example of OPEC and NIEO shows that in international relations cooperation and conflict are but opposite sides of the same coin. The very success of OPEC so far has bred division among its members as to what the next step should be with Saudi Arabia taking a relatively cautious and conservative view as against that of the more militant oil-producers, such as Libya. Again, the oil crisis has driven the deepest wedges into the group of developing countries as a whole. The poorer among them, being vitally dependent upon oil for their development hopes, have been if anything more hard hit by the oil policies of OPEC than the industrialized states. And the industrialized states themselves, though driven together by their common plight at the receiving end of OPEC price policies, have - or rather some of them have - found it expedient to settle with the oil producers unilaterally on the best terms available. In Britain's case, the prospects opened up for her by the discovery of oil in the North Sea have for the time being put her on the side of OPEC as an oil producer and against her fellow industrialized states. The whole relationship, in other words, between developed and developing countries and between members of these two groups inter se, seems to show that while economic needs, as they loom larger in a nation's thinking, make international cooperation more necessary, they can also make it more difficult.

As for the industrialized countries, the international character of their economic problems has been abundantly evident during the period of recession in the 1970s; their problems have been similar from one country to another. The indices of their economic performance have tended to move together, and the hopes of recovery for any one of them are clearly dependent upon the economic state of all the rest. The present recession began with the dramatic weakening of the dollar in August, 1971. At a meeting in London in May 1977, the seven major Western industrial nations rightly concluded that they must look to one another to take measures which would collectively expand production, markets, and the demand for labor. That sense of sharing a common predicament was evident in the seven pledges for concerted action which the summit meeting adopted in its final declaration. (11) But it could also be said that the meeting brought out the fundamental differences between these seven nations almost as much as it drove home the need for coordinating their policies. Broadly speaking, the rift lay between the weaker economies among the seven, notably those of Britain, Italy, and, to a lesser extent, France, and the stronger, notably those of Federal Germany, Japan, and the United States. The weaker group wanted the stronger to step up their rate of economic growth in order to create more markets for themselves, while the stronger counted themselves lucky to be avoiding the inflation suffered by the weaker states and accordingly wished to keep their reflation in check. In that situation, in which there is no force apart from common interest to bring about harmonized policies, the most states can do is to exhort other countries to mend their ways. However, it is entirely up to those other countries to decide whether or not to comply, and the making of that decision may not be entirely in the hands of the government. A few months after this May meeting, Mr. Callaghan, the British Prime Minister, observed that the seven pledges the meeting committed itself to did not seem to have been kept.

We can now move from this general comment on how economic needs and policies may affect the outlook for international cooperation and consider some of the specific ways in which those needs and policies can make the coordination of national foreign policies harder. Four types of situation may be examined. One is where a country's adverse balance-of-payments position gives rise to internal demands for the imposition of import controls, usually defended as "temporary," in order to protect jobs and wages; as a parallel policy, a country urges trade competitors to take measures which will have the effect of reducing the sale of their exports in the home market or in foreign markets in which the home country's goods are competitive. Trade restrictions of this kind may, in the classic theory of international economics, tend to limit the total world volume of purchasing power and hence, in the long run, the demand for the goods of all countries. Of course, that sort of argument is likely to sound abstract and remote to the worker threatened by the loss of his job. Even though the goods he helps produce are being edged out of world markets by a competitor, it may be politically expedient for his country to remain on good terms with that competitor.

The second economic context in which the coordination of the foreign policies of states may prove difficult is where there is competition for limited, or seemingly limited, resources. The energy example is an obvious one: as industrialization proceeds around the world and population grows, so will the demand for energy, especially oil, with its essentially limited supply and apparently low substitutability. In theory, scientific research should be capable of discovering and making available to mankind ever new forms of power. However, the production of these new forms often demands basic raw materials which are in short supply as compared with need, or, as in the case of nuclear energy, the production is attended with hazards, biological or political, or both. Moreover, when scientific research does cover hitherto unknown sources of wealth, as for instance in the bed of the sea, it has been found not so much that this gives further scope for international cooperation in the exploitation of the new wealth, but that jealousies and mutual fears are engendered as the nations jostle with each other to earmark claims to the new resources. It is interesting in this connection to see how the Greeks and Turks, whose mutual animosities have been so persistent over the history of the international system, have found new matters to quarrel about in the prospects of oil and other mineral resources in the bed of the Aegean Sea. When, in 1976, Turkey sent a research ship, Sizmik I, to explore the Aegean seabed, a critical level of tension was reached between Ankara and Athens.

Here, again, there is an obvious contradiction between what may be called the logic and the politics of the situation. On the face of it, nations would seem to have more to gain by combining their efforts in exploiting and using to better advantage the fruits of the earth than by sequestrating a portion of them and jealously exploiting that portion unilaterally. However, joint efforts are advantages which have a general abstract aspect, and tend to make themselves felt in the long run rather than in the here and now. They are something like the benefits of price stability which the British government at present promises the trade unions if they show restraint in making wage demands. This smacks of "pie in the sky," when compared with the fatter and more visible wage packet which enables a bigger basket of goods to be bought even though the prices of those goods may rise to restore the original real income later.

Above all we must remember the all-too-vital politics of international cooperation in this matter of resource allocation. Government ministers at an international conference may no doubt sincerely wish to stand forth as models of altruism and fair dealing, and may sincerely believe that the human race as a whole must benefit, though possibly only "at the end of the day," from the equitable division of natural resources among the different nations according to their size and need. But such ministers can only hope to retain their people's support, and therefore to continue to attend international conferences as their country's spokesmen, so long as people at home believe that they can "deliver the goods" in the form of speedy increments to their living standards. Ministers returning home and telling their country's press that they fought at the conference for fairness and justice but the other country got the contract can hardly expect popular support. This political aspect of the emphasis placed today on national economic achievement is no doubt intensified by the stress laid by government departments, the mass media, employers' federations, and trade unions on national statistics of economic performance, graphs of output of various sorts of goods, charts of price indices, wage levels, profits, and interest rates. Before 1939, no doubt most people in Europe and North America had some inkling what the "national income" meant, and hoped that, for their own countries, it was growing annually. People did not assume that national wealth ought to be growing by some appreciable percentage year by year, and they did not write their countries off as failures if it did not. Today, ministers in most countries seem to live in a veritable sea of graphs pinpointing at regular intervals the exact state of health of every sector of the national economy. If the statistics show that national output is not on an upward curve, if the worker and housewife are not better off this year than last year, the minister is summoned before the television cameras to explain the reason, much like a doctor called to the bed of an irascible patient wanting to know why the temperature chart shows a rise when he expects a decline. Not surprisingly, the minister, or any other national representative, who repeatedly has to face this ordeal by statistics finds that he simply cannot afford to deal with other countries in any other way than one which will improve the government's position in the charts, or at least prevent it from getting worse.

This, then, is the third way in which the economic stress in contemporary international politics can complicate the diplomatic process. Generally speaking, and contrary to what many people seem to think, the minister and diplomat have little interest in seeing international negotiation fail or make only slow progress. It is surely better for them to have something to report than nothing, or so at least the achievement-oriented Western diplomat would appear to think. Plainly, the greater and more varied the demands emanating from within a country on the government, the harder becomes its task of bringing back from abroad what looks like solid benefits for its constituents, and the more disadvantageous it is to return home with nothing to show from so much talk with the foreigner. In days when such vague things as "national honor" and "national glory" were what the state's representatives were supposed to defend in their missions abroad, a certain amount of bombastic talk might serve to secure their credibility at home. When the question is "How many Concordes have we sold this year?" or "Did we get the contract to build the air-raid warning system for that Middle East state?", it is far more difficult for a government and its officials to get by with bluffing.

This leads finally to the fourth area in which a clash may be discerned between a state's economic objectives in foreign policy and its ability to cooperate in the common interest with other states. We are thinking here of the economic aspect of defense, and in particular of collective defense systems of the sort legalized by Article 51 of the United Nations Charter and represented by NATO and the Warsaw Treaty Organization (WTO). It is significant that the New Nationalism, in the sense of an increased concern of the nations with economic achievement and economic welfare, has tended to coincide with the so-called detente in East-West relations. This began in the early 1960s, though there was some evidence of it as early as March 1953 following the death of Stalin. The coincidence of the two developments - the

New Nationalism and the East-West detente - is not, of course, surprising. The danger of world war receded with the detente, and nations, especially the aligned nations, began to feel that there was more to life - the enjoyment of affluence, for instance - than being permanently on guard against aggression; and, on the other side, the increasing interest of ordinary people in higher living standards may have driven governments of the aligned nations to soften the asperity of the East-West conflict in order to give their people a little more of what they fancied. However that may be, the New Nationalism certainly placed a strain on collective defense organizations, as the allied people began to realize that the higher the costs of national defense, the smaller the portion of the national cake available for civilian needs. The burden of defense in collective organizations such as NATO has always been unwelcome to taxpayers, although it is not as heavy as the defense burden carried by some non-aligned states such as Israel and Syria. The burden can come to seem even greater when the international climate takes a turn for the better as it has with the detente. When the East-West arms race continues despite the detente, people are puzzled. Partly as a consequence of the New Nationalism, the good life - in the strictly material sense of the term - has become for them the supreme value and should be the chief objective of their governments as well. We will return to this general point in the next section.

Before coming to that aspect of the subject, however, it is proper to restate the main theme of the present section. When we consider the impact of the New Nationalism, as we have defined it, on the perennial problem of international relations, that is, the coordination of the foreign policies of the different states, we see that this impact is in some ways ambivalent and self-contradictory. On the one hand, as the planet gets more crowded and production grows, as the economic links and relationships between the nation-states multiply, as the economic needs of states and the demands on governments increase, it becomes steadily more clear that no state can "go it alone" today, if it ever could. All states are thickly enmeshed in a network of international linkages, public and private, institutionalized and casual, economic and social, as well as political and strategic, which span the globe. Every state must be continuously in communication with other states, especially its immediate neighbors, and must try, freshly every day, to hammer out the terms on which it will live with them. However, that is far from being the end of the story; it is really only the beginning. The need to coordinate policies with other states, it cannot be emphasized too much, does not mean that coordination is possible, certainly not that it is easy. On the contrary, it might even be said that the more pressing the need for coordinating policies in the international system, the more difficult it becomes.

THE NORTH ATLANTIC COMMUNITY AND THE
NEW NATIONALISM

The North Atlantic regional defense system, based on the North Atlantic Treaty signed in Washington on April 4, 1949 and now embracing 15 European and North American nations, took shape before the New Nationalism really began to make itself felt. The 1949 Treaty and the organization, NATO, which grew up on the basis of the treaty, were in effect responses to the feelings of insecurity among the North Atlantic democratic states resulting from uncertainty as to how far west in Europe the Soviet government proposed to extend its influence and authority. These feelings were heightened after the conversion of Czechoslovakia into a Communist state in February 1948, and after the Soviet blockade of the western sector of Berlin later the same year. The essential bases of the Atlantic collective defense system built up thereafter were, on the one hand, the determination of American politicians to use all their national power to ensure that western Europe should not fall under Communist control, and the equal determination of the major non-Communist west European states, joined in 1951 by Greece and Turkey, to organize their collective defense within a framework mainly provided, at least in the early years, by American military (including nuclear) and economic strength.

It soon became evident that this Atlantic military solidarity could not be effective in the fullest sense without progress toward integration, or some degree of it, in three other areas between member-states: the economic, the political, and, for want of a better term, the cultural or ideological. Economic cooperation, as Article 2 of the treaty made clear, was necessary in order to develop the economic muscle behind an increasingly costly military effort, and to ensure that unnecessary conflict in economic policies would be eliminated. Political cooperation was required so that the alliance might present as much of a common front as it could in negotations with the Soviet Union on such issues as Berlin and a divided Germany, so that the alliance could face the really critical questions of war and peace with a common mind, as far as possible, and so that political disputes between member-states would not jeopardize the general unit of the alliance. Lastly, it was important on the cultural or ideological level that the political principles which the alliance was forged to defend should be widely understood in member-states in order that their peoples would be willing to make the efforts and sacrifices needed for collective defense. The pledge in Article 2 of the original treaty to bring about "a better understanding of the principles upon which these (free) institutions are founded" reflects this.

In spite of all this, it cannot be said that integration in the Atlantic system, outside the military and naval spheres, has progressed very far. The hopes expressed by many politicians on both sides of the Atlantic in the 1950s and 1960s concerning the development of some kind of Atlantic community, with institutions for joint action, and possibly with federation or con- federation as the ultimate outcome, have remained mostly stillborn. (12) Economic collaboration between the 15 Atlantic nations is certainly close and continuous, but this tends to be more visible within the Organization for Economic Cooperation and Development (OECD), which has a wider member- ship, than in NATO. There is no doubt that OECD would proceed among such rich and powerful nations even if NATO did not exist. Again, political cooperation is certainly active and continuous among the 15 Atlantic nations. The regular sessions of the NATO Council, as well as the customary informal diplomatic contacts, are symbolic of this. Still there is little sign, if any, of the NATO Council developing into anything more than the traditional diplomatic conference for coordinating essentially separate foreign policies. In particular, there is no suggestion whatsoever of any Atlantic nation being willing, at present or in the immediate future, to abandon its basic sovereign right to say "No" when resolutions of the NATO Council are drafted for the approval of the 15 nations.   As for the idea of a common cultural effort among NATO member-states, the whole essence of their character as democratic communities would seem to be against it, if what is intended is anything more than the encouragement in one another's countries of the periodic discussion of common problems without commitments.

It might even be argued that integration - meaning some real surrender to central organs of the right of member states to decide their internal and external policies - has become even more of a non-starter in the Atlantic system since, say, the mid-1950s.   The subject is certainly less discussed in public than it was in the active years of Clarence Streit, the best-known proponent of Atlantic union, and the reasons for this are quite clear.   The disparity between the power, and hence the policies, of the United States and her European allies has impressively increased in recent years, as evidenced by the Vietnam War, the development of a bilateral American detente with, respectively, the Soviet Union and China, and the formidable growth in America's independent nuclear power which led to the exclusion of her European allies from talks on strategic arms (SALT) with the Soviet Union. On the side of the European allies, the presidency of Charles de Gaulle in France (1958-69), and the legacy which this left for France and other West European foreign policies, dimmed the hopes of anything in the way of political fusion between the allies on both sides of the Atlantic. It is possible too that, contrary to early expectations in NATO circles, the process of building the European Communities, in itself agonizingly slow, has served to divert the attention and energies of the European allies away from the integration process in NATO.   There is no doubt, however, especially with the recent apparent strengthening of Warsaw Pact forces and the renewed debate in East-West relations about human rights, that convictions about the necessity for the NATO deterrent structure remain as strong as ever among the allies.   But these have hardly been matched by the feeling that this demands some early progress toward fusing the separate sovereignties of member-states.   Even in the military field, the many continuing difficulties in the standardization of equipment are dramatic testimony to the persistence of national particularism.   There are few indications that the NATO alliance, within any foreseeable future, is likely to take on anything like the form of a single, amalgamated state, especially if the East-West detente prospers.

Above and beyond all this, we have to consider to what extent the New Nationalism, as we have defined it, has affected and is affecting the coordination of national foreign policies in the Atlantic Community. First of all, it is clear that, if we assume that a new sort of nationalism, which for the sake of convenience we call the New Nationalism, has indeed come into existence, it has not made the coordination of policies in NATO conspicuously easier.   Outside the military field that coordination is as hard to achieve today as it ever was, if not harder.   It is true that, at the present time (November 1977), the American administration under President Carter seems more sensitive to the opinions of allies than the former Nixon-Ford-Kissinger team, and that the disintegrative influence of de Gaulle has left the scene; these are perhaps the passing consequences of chance and personality. The seeming consensus among the seven western industrial nations at their economic conference in London in May 1977, though welcome after the divisiveness of the Nixon-Kissinger era, certainly seemed short-lived. Again, we must conclude, the Atlantic governments' worries about economic problems may make them cast anxiously about for international remedies; but, having found and tried some, they still seem to think that in the last resort the big decisions, whether in the maintenance of full employment, the reduction of inflation, or the increase in national output and wealth are for themselves to make individually.

It is here that we reach the ultimate, and most dangerous, paradox: namely, that, in their search to satisfy the economic and social aspirations of their peoples, democratic governments are bound to be led into courses which are harmful to military alliances, such as NATO, which were created for the defense of their territory and their political independence. The most critical form this takes, of course, is the conflict between standards of living and consumer expenditure, and spending on defense. In one sense, there is no conflict for defense spending keeps people in jobs. Any disbanding of NATO or disarmament of its member-states would clearly mean unemployment, at least until, if ever, workers were transferred to non-military enterprises. In the more immediate run things are not nearly so obvious. With inflation rampant in almost all NATO states and with punishing rates of taxation, the politician cannot but try to win votes by promises of cuts in defense spending. These are popular promises at the current time when the immediate risk of war on the central front between East and West has dramatically receded, if not totally disappeared. The decision of the NATO Council summit meeting in London in May 1977 to increase defense spending by 3% seems more a brave gesture than a real reversal of the inroad made by the New Nationalism into the collective alliance effort.

It is one of the many paradoxical truths about NATO that the more it succeeds in making the danger of war remote, the less the people of its member-states seem to regard it as necessary. There is not very much that NATO governments can do to correct this, apart from stressing the contribution of collective defense to peace, since they themselves must echo the popular argument against it if they are going to hold on to power. Fortunately, the Communist world can be relied upon to act as a continuing advocate of defense spending by the NATO states through its conspicuous efforts to pull abreast of and to exceed the West in practically all forms of military capability.

CONCLUSION

The conclusion of this paper is that there is indeed in the world today a New Nationalism in the sense that the nations of the late twentieth century seem rather more united by a common interest in social and economic advancement than by traditional ideas of national glory and expansion. All governments today must to a greater or lesser extent reflect this New Nationalism by adding to the older goals of foreign policy these newer social and political objectives. Further, while the New Nationalism is perhaps rather more favorable to international peace than the old, and while it obliges governments to face the necessity of contacts and cooperation with other states, it cannot be said to make that task, or the general coordination of the policies of the different states any easier, if easier at all. In particular, the pressure on governments to be always improving the lot of their people is bound to give a competitive, perhaps sometimes bitter, edge to their work in the arena of international cooperation. The North Atlantic system cannot be said to have escaped the effects of this New Nationalism. Since its raison d'etre is the provision of necessarily costly military defense, there is bound to be some conflict between this and the satisfaction of the social and economic objectives of present-day national governments.

One solution to the problem is, of course, education. The administration of a modern state is a highly complex business, and people have to understand how one set of demands on the administration has to be balanced with all the others. The British people are learning to do this, or must learn to do this, in quite another sphere, that is, the balancing of wage and salary demands (all of which may be legitimate in their own way) with the overall public interest in combating inflation and maintaining full employment. To accustom oneself to the need for balancing the immediate national interest against the more remote international interest is vastly more difficult, but that nevertheless is what the people of the different countries must learn to do.

Secondly, we should empty our minds of the easy-going but misleading idea that interdependence in the international system necessarily dictates mutual cooperation and a spirit of compromise. Often it has merely the reverse effect. Two armies locked in conflict on the battlefield are also "interdependent" in the sense that each one is reacting directly to the moves of the other. The same condition of conflictual interdependence can exist in the world of economic life, and the more aware we are of this fact the more likely we are to be able to control the conflict.

Lastly, the dimensions of this problem are likely to be completely transformed with the economic advance of the now developing countries and the concomitant increase in their political power which will inevitably go with it. We have seen some early signs of this in the crisis of oil prices since 1973 and in the recent demand of the developing countries for a New International Economic Order. So far the technicalities of international cooperation and the coordination of foreign policies have tended to be discussed by Europeans and North Americans in the context of the older and richer nation-states, and that indeed is the spirit of the present paper. However, this world is rapidly being swallowed up in a vastly greater world made up mostly of developing countries agitated by their problems, interests, and policies. The effect of this new order could be to drive the older, developed states into a self-defensive league of their own, in which case the coordination of policies among them might be less of a problem than in the past, or the effect could be to divide them. What is clear beyond doubt is that the problem of coordinating the separate foreign policies of separate states will remain with us so long as the present structure of the international political system exists.

NOTES

(1) See, among many such works, Andrew Scott, The Revolution in Statecraft: Informal Penetration (New York: Random House, 1965); and Robert O. Keohane and Joseph S. Nye (Eds.), Transnational Relations and World Politics (Cambridge, Mass.: Harvard University Press) 1970 and 1971.

(2) J.H. Herz, "Rise and Demise of the Territorial State," World Politics, July 1957, which was subsequently worked up into a book, International Politics in the Atomic Age (New York: Columbia University Press) 1959. Herz later revised his review of the demise of the nation-state.

(3) UN Charter, Article, 1(3), 12(1b), Chapters IX and X.

(4) F.P. Walters, A History of the League of Nations (London: OUP, 1952), Vol. I, pp. 761-2.

(5) James N. Rosenau (ed.), Linkage Politics: Essays on the Convergence of National and International Systems (New York: The Free Press, 1969).

(6) See William Wallace, The Foreign Policy Process in Britain (London: OUP, 1975), for some interesting examples from modern British practice.

(7) Published by Her Majesty's Stationery Office, London.

(8) Francis Delaisi, Political Myths and Economic Realities (London: Douglas, 1925).

(9) Harold and Margaret Sprout, Towards a Politics of Planet Earth (New York: VanNostrand, 1971).

(10) Gamani Corea, "UNCTAD and the International Economic Order," International Affairs (London: RIIA, April, 1977).

(11) The Times, May 9, 1977.

(12) See the account of the integration process in the North Atlantic system given by Elliot R. Goodman in The Fate of the Atlantic Community (New York: Praeger, 1975).

4 Coordinating Foreign Policies: Problems Within the Atlantic Alliance
Wolfram F. Hanrieder

INTRODUCTION

The forces of nationalism, aside from the inhibitions created by the nuclear balance, have proved to be the major restraint placed upon the conduct of the super-powers in the period after World War II. In their attempt to create a world order congenial to their ideological preferences or to their national interest, both the United States and the Soviet Union have had to contend with the stubborn appeal of nationalism, within as well as outside of their respective alliances. The fissures appearing in both the North Atlantic Treaty Organization and the Warsaw Treaty Organization during the last two decades are in large part attributable to the resistance on the part of secondary alliance members to make their policies conform to the guidelines set forth by their respective alliance super-powers. In many instances, this resistance was based not so much on ideological grounds - nationalism as a counter-ideology to trans-national ideologies - but on pragmatic considerations which seemed to suggest that pronounced differences among national socio-economic and political circumstances warranted divergent paths toward a desirable social order. The New Nationalism of the last decades, although not lacking in emotional overtones, was largely based on rational calculations on how to further the national interest within a global configuration of power (and its regional manifestations) in which the super-powers exerted an overwhelming measure of influence.

The exasperation with which both the United States and the Soviet Union have in the past responded to deviationists within their alliances attests to the intractable problems that national divergencies have posed for the streamlining and coordination of policies within alliances. The fact that the United States and the Soviet Union have, in practical terms, responded differently to the challenges of nationalism within their alliances does not alter the fact that both Moscow and Washington have sought to contain the centrifugal tendencies within their spheres of influence as much as possible.

Moreover, the United States at least has viewed the problems experienced by the Soviet Union in Eastern Europe with a measure of guarded sympathy. The much-noted remarks by Helmut Sonnenfeldt in December 1975,* in which he suggested that the present relationship between the Soviet Union and Eastern Europe was "unnatural" and "inorganic" and therefore could prove destabilizing and a threat to world peace, seem to indicate that the United States perceived the forces of nationalism to be detrimental to American interests even if they were operative in the opponent's sphere of influence. To what extent Moscow's hostile reaction to Euro-communism stems from a similar calculation is of course a matter of speculation.

Both super-powers also have had considerable difficulty in dealing with the forces of nationalism in the Third World. Many of these new states, and some older ones as well, are going through a process of self-definition. In their quest for a viable statehood, the governing elites in these new states have used the rhetoric and symbolism of nationalism to create or enhance a national identity that is ill-defined, if not entirely lacking. Many of these states have achieved juridical recognition of statehood in advance of their capacities to perform as states. It is not surprising that the elites in these states seek to enhance national consciousness and the corresponding legitimation of their rule by stressing the notions of separateness, of a distinct identity, that are inherent in the ideology of nationalism. This also explains in part the lack of success of trans-national ideologies in many Third World states. Aside from the dubious relevance of ideological prescriptions in dealing with immediate problems of governance, adherence to trans-national ideologies would diminish the measure of independence and separateness that these states have achieved only in the recent past. Although the governments of some of these countries describe themselves as Marxist or socialist, there is little indication that this means adherence to an internationalist Marxist ideology. Any trans-national or cosmopolitan value system is bound to have limited appeal to new states that are engaged in the process of self-definition which is perceived primarily in national terms. The Soviet experience in Egypt, Cuba, and in several African countries has demonstrated that the Soviet Union is at least as inept as the United States in attempting to steer political and economic development in the Third World on the basis of ideological prescriptions. By and large, both the Soviet Union and the United States have persistently and seriously underestimated the forces of national- ism in their dealings with the Third World. American opposition throughout the late 1950s and 1960s to the so-called neutralism of the Third World was based in large part on a misreading of the psychological and political factors that motivated the elites in Third World countries. Only most recently, and belatedly, has the American position shifted to the extent that Secretary of State Cyrus Vance could argue that American policies should recognize and encourage African nationalism. Also, at least part of the reason for the American debacle in Vietnam (aside from the futile attempt to apply measures of containment that had proved successful in Europe to areas in which they were totally inappropriate) was a misreading of the driving forces and appeal of nationalism in Southeast Asia. Ho Chi Minh was as much a nationalist as he was a communist, and the war in Vietnam was a war of

---

* "Sonnenfeldt Doctrine"

reunification as much as a war of ideology. As John Lewis Gaddis has put it, "compared to such entrenched phenomena as nationalism, racism, greed, or sheer human intractability, communism is today a relatively insignificant determinant of events on the international scene, unless of course we choose to impart significance to it by giving it more attention than it deserves." (1)

NATIONALISM AND INTERDEPENDENCE

Nationalism, then, is alive and well. Far from being secondary and obsolete phenomena, nationalism and the idea of the national interest are central elements in contemporary world politics, and the international system has remained an interstate system in some of its essential features. But at the same time equally powerful forces are at work in contemporary international politics which have curtailed or in any case modified the role of the nation-state. These developments - usually summarized by the term interdependence - are in part the result of the changing nature of the nation-state itself and in part the result of new ways in which nation-states interact.

A number of years ago John Herz argued in a much-noted article that for centuries the major attribute of the nation-state was its "territoriality": its identification with an area that was surrounded by a "wall of defensibility" and hence relatively impermeable to outside penetration. This territoriality was bound to vanish, so Herz argued, largely because of developments in the means of destruction, such as nuclear weapons, which made even the most powerful nation-state subject to being penetrated. (2) Although Herz later modified his views on the impending demise of the nation-state, his previous argument on the changing meaning and importance of territoriality was clearly valid. Territorial occupancy or acquisition by and large is not a pressing issue in contemporary international politics: access rather than acquisition, presence rather than rule, penetration rather than possession have become the important questions. Aside from political and economic implications, this development has significantly changed the meaning of military security and the utility of military capabilities. Phenomena such as invasions and military aggression have to be re-examined in light of the diminishing importance of territorial possession, especially in areas such as Western Europe which are basically unattractive objects of physical aggression and territorial occupation.

Another major change in the nature of the nation-state has been its growing responsiveness to what Daniel Bell calls the "revolution of rising entitlement."(3) Modern governments have become increasingly sensitive to the demand by citizens for a wide variety of welfare services and have taken on the responsibility for mass social and economic welfare. The improvement, through state intervention, of the material well-being of its citizens has become one of the central functions of state activity, and the satisfaction of rising claims by citizens has become the major element in the state's legitimation. This development has led to an increasing flow of interactions, of social demand-and-supply communications, between the state and society. Politics rather than the market has become the major agent for the redistribution of wealth and power.

This vertical interaction between government and society has been complemented by increasing horizontal interaction between the units of world politics on the government-to-government level. This increased interaction is taking place in bilateral as well as multilateral dimensions, in government-to-government transactions as well as in the context of international organizations and directorates.

The distinction between vertical and horizontal interactions, popularized by several authors, needs to be supplemented, however, by two additional types of processes. Another increase in interactions has developed that might be labeled "lateral" interaction. Sub-national groups and organizations, such as multinational business firm agreements, international banking and invest-ment activities, the coordinating and consultative arrangements among national parties, dialogues among labor unions, and the activities of international guerilla organizations are examples of this type of interaction.

Another distinct process of interaction is "integrative," involving supra-national agencies and economic-integrative mechanisms, such as the Euro-pean Common Market, which are characterized by some measure of institutionalization and have to some extent diminished national sovereignty.

In sum, what has developed is an interconnected flow of national (vertical), international (horizontal), trans-national (lateral), and supra-national (integrative) forces: a complex of relationships which is usually described as interdependence, in which demands are articulated and processed through institutional as well as informal channels.

Five consequences of these developments are important for our purposes. First, in seeking to satisfy the demands brought to the government from within society on the vertical level of interaction, government has to rely on the other three levels; domestic demands can only be satisfied by partici-pation in international, trans-national, or integrative activities. Governments are increasingly pushed toward the international arena for satisfying the rising flow of domestic demands created by the welfare state.

> Domestic governments lie at the nexus of vertical and horizontal interaction. They are impelled in one direction by the desire to satisfy the electorate and to build domestic support. They are impelled in another by the high degree of horizontal integration of the system. If governments are to satisfy the demands of the electorate in economic and financial policies, they may have to cooperate more fully with other nations. Under the stimulus of economic nationalism, however, nations may also occasionally act against the multilateral framework (But).... if nationalistic goals depend on supportive actions by other members of the international community, nationalism cannot be achieved in isolation. (4)

A second point is that the resolution of domestic political conflicts over the redistribution of wealth and power takes place in a wider context, one that reaches into the areas of lateral, integrative, and horizontal processes. This has an effect on the outcome of conflict. As E. E. Schattschneider has put it: "The outcome of all conflict is determined by the <u>scope</u> of its contagion. The number of people involved in any conflict determines what happens; every change in the number of participants, every increase or reduction in the number of participants affects the result." (5) This process depends of course on the extent to which national governments permit lateral processes to take place. If lateral or integrative processes are curtailed by governmental restrictions, the scope of conflict will be curtailed.

The third point is the corollary of the second. Because of the inter-penetration of domestic and international-trans-national-integrative processes, political conflict is not only projected from the domestic onto the international scene but international conflicts over redistribution of income are projected onto domestic political scenes. National governments have always been at the fulcrum where foreign and domestic policies meet, where they have to be weighed and adjusted, and where the perennial scarcity of resources compels hard choices and rank-ordering of priority. (6) Govern-ments have to deal with two interlocking processes of redistribution of power, influence and wealth. In most contemporary societies, and in previous ones as well, the government presides over a continuous process of redistribution of wealth and influence on the domestic scene. It does so whether it is an activist government with a conscious commitment to redistribution through, say, progressive taxation, or whether it is content to let market forces make the redistribution. A redistribution of wealth and influence takes place in either case. By not acting, the government acts. At the same time, a national government, facing the international environment, is confronted with an equally continuous redistribution process in the international system, a constantly shifting balance of power arrangements.

A fourth point is that the distinction between high politics and low politics - popularized by a number of analysts - should be redefined and sharpened. The implied dichotomy between the pursuit of security and power (the dramatic-political-intangible) and the pursuit of welfare and affluence (the economic-incremental-tangible) can be overdrawn of course. Karl Kaiser was correct when he suggested a number of years ago that what political actors view as either high or low politics depends on specific circumstances, changes over time, and differences from country to country. (7) There is, however, an element of distinction between high and low politics that has not been sufficiently stressed and that is pertinent to my argument: power, security, and defense commodities are indivisible, and hence less subject to the redistributive aspects of political processes, whereas welfare issues are divisible, and hence at the very core of redistribution politics. In short, goals such as power and security are public goods and subject to the calculus of relative gain, whereas goals pertaining to welfare, economics and profit are private goods and can be assessed with respect to absolute gain. To put it another way: high politics pertain to indivisible, collective goods whereas low politics pertain to divisible, private goods.

Fifth, the interaction and interdependence operative in these processes is possible only in a certain type of international system that allows it. "Liberalization," minimal interference with trade, investment, and other sorts of communications are essential in order for horizontal, lateral, and integrative processes to take place. By and large it can be argued that the

United States has encouraged the development of this type of international environment, as much as possible, in the decades following World War II. Although America's dominant position in this system has been seriously eroded, the United States was the major architect of the postwar economic and monetary systems. International economic systems, as much as military-strategic and political systems, reflect the influence and policies of the predominant powers in the system. The international economic system of the postwar period was essentially the creation of the United States. Although conceived initially as a global, universal system of liberalized trade and monetary relations, following the onset of the Cold War the international economic system eventually began to revolve around the trilateral relationship among the United States, Western Europe, and Japan, with the Communist economic system becoming a regional sub-system. This trilateral economic system of the major centers of non-communist industrial power was subjected to increasing stress during the 1960s, and underwent major changes in the early 1970s. The net effect of these changes was that the United States has had to share its predominant position with Europe and Japan, leading to a new international monetary and trading system whose shape is still uncertain and ambiguous and further complicated by the monetary resources that have become available to OPEC countries.(8)

What is at work then is a development in which international politics become subject to a process of domestication. The more international political processes become characterized by activities that are distributive-divisible-tangible, the more they resemble traditional domestic processes of redistribution. This development is fed from two mutually reinforcing sources. On the one hand, the diminishing salience of security issues relative to economic issues, to territorial acquisition, and to trans-national ideologies signifies a narrowing of the area of high, non-distributive politics and a corresponding enlargement of the area of low, distributive politics. In short, non-distributive political processes are giving way to distributive processes, expressed largely in economic terms. At the same time, distributive processes have increased in frequency as well as in intensity - intra-nationally-vertically as well as internationally-horizontally and trans-nationally - laterally - giving rise to the phenomenon usually described as interdependence. Since governments rely on horizontal and lateral trans-actions to meet demands made on them in vertical domestic demand processes, distributive political activities on the international and national levels have become intermingled.

It is the very domestication of international politics, however, which restores in some important ways the vitality of the nation-state. It isn't so much that international welfare issues have emerged as high politics, as some authors woud suggest, but rather that distributive political processes have gained in relative importance, and that the demands generated within a society can no longer be satisfied without recourse to trans-national processes. This has led to ironic consequences. Analysts such as John Herz, as well as many of the so-called neo-functionalists, perceived the major change in international political, economic, and strategic processes to come from a gradual weakening of the nation-state. Trans-national processes, either integrative or otherwise penetrative, were expected to modify the nation-state. Modern international politics were to dissolve the nation-state. What has happened, however, is that the new nation-state has "dissolved" a certain type of international politics by diminishing (relatively) the importance of non-distributive processes and enhancing the importance of distributive processes. (9)

Another ironic consequence is what has happened to the term "national interest." The concept of the national interest is, practically by definition, an idea based on non-distributive, indivisible values enjoyed by society as a whole: security, prestige and advantages sought by manipulating the balance of power. As international politics become more and more "domesticated," the areas covered by the concept of the national interest become narrower and more ambiguous. Distributive value, unlike indivisible values, are not shared equally by all segments of society. Since the idea of the nation-state and the national interest have been used in an almost symbiotic sense, at least in traditional parlance, it seems indeed ironic that while the salience of the nation-state has in many respects been enhanced, for the reasons enumerated, the salience of the term "national interest" has been diminished or, at the very least, has become highly ambiguous. (10)

"DOMESTICATION" PATTERNS OF INTERNATIONAL POLITICS

In a more differentiated way, what does "domestication" of international politics mean? What domestic model of political and economic processes, of what state or what type of state, is being approximated by international processes? What type of nation-state "dissolves" traditional international politics?

The Third World

One type of domestic order that is clearly not approximated by the general international system is that of a typical Third World country - if one may use such terms as "typical" in this context. One of the most fundamental differences between developed and underdeveloped societies is the difference between their domestic redistributive demand structures: the way in which demands are generated, articulated, aggregated, and conveyed to governmental structures for satisfaction. Less developed countries (LDCs) generally have few viable sub-national institutions that can effectively articulate demands both vertically and laterally, within as well as outside of their political systems. These systems are "state-dominant" systems rather than "society-dominant" systems because their institutional and bureaucratic structures are intended primarily to administer governmental demands rather than respond to societal demands. Vertical interaction is fragmentary and erratic in both directions. Lateral interaction is by and large impossible because no viable sub-governmental organizations exist that could fulfill such functions and interact with sub-governmental structures in other societies. One result is that the redistributive demands made on the international scene have to be made, by and large, by the governments of the LDCs. To put it another way, these demands are articulated by the state rather than by society, horizontally rather than laterally.

Moreover, in those LDCs that have emerged only recently from colonial domination, many of which are characterized by artificial borders and strong centrifugal forces, it is only natural that their governments should emphasize, in their quest for self-definition, the cohesive rather than the potentially disintegrative features of their system. In this situation, a state's legitimacy is much more effectively asserted through its foreign than through its domestic policies. The reality of a new nation, its uniqueness and integrity are more easily expressed in its external relations than in divisive domestic political processes. This type of political process is also exemplified in the fact that territorial disputes are by and large limited to this type of social system.

In many LDCs this entire process toward statism is reinforced by the establishment of an administrative new class, whose political activities are in no way revolutionary in the sense of leading toward a fundamentally restructured social order or creating one de novo. In the absence of a broad middle class, these elites have become conservative, turning themselves into an administrative bourgeoisie. (11) All this supports the view that the political and economic dealings of the LDCs tend to be state-managed and consequently focused on horizontal rather than lateral trans-national processes, and that demands for redistribution of income on the international level also have to be articulated on a government-to-government level. In Daniel Bell's words, "The international political arena becomes the cockpit for overt economic demands by the 'external proletariat' (to use Toynbee's phrase) of the world against the richer industrial nations." (12)

The Soviet and Chinese Model

Neither does the prevailing "domestication" of international politics approximate the Soviet or Chinese model. The parallels between the Third World model and the Soviet and Chinese models are obvious. Although there are, of course, significant differences between the Third World state model and those of the Soviet Union and the People's Republic of China, neither the Soviet Union nor China has managed to "export" its internal redistribution demand structures on a global scale; and the Soviet Union has had only tentative and incomplete success in exporting its model to its sphere of influence, Eastern Europe. Space limitations do not permit a fuller exploration of the differences, as well as parallels, that characterize the relevant structures in the Soviet Union, Communist China, and typical Third World countries. It could be demonstrated, however, that the prevailing "domestication" of international politics is not the result of Soviet or Chinese political and economic activities, and in fact has placed the Soviet Union and Communist China at a tremendous disadvantage relative to the economic power of the trilateral, industrialized world.

The Industrialized Trilateral Model

It is apparent that the domestication of international politics follows a paradigm that stems from the internal processes of highly developed industrialized societies, primarily those of the United States, Japan, and Western and Northern Europe. These processes are characterized by a high frequency and intensity of internal vertical interaction as well as horizontal and lateral interactions, and by the prevalence of demands which might be summarized by the term "middle class." These countries are not only similar with respect to the types of demands that percolate within and among them, but they also have available to them a similar set of policy instruments with which to direct, contain, expand, or otherwise affect both vertical-domestic as well as horizontal-international and lateral-trans-national processes: trade and monetary policy, fiscal policy, income policy, wages policy, labor policy, taxation policy.   There is a wide array of instruments with which modern governments and their bureaucracies can manipulate national as well as international demand flows; similar functions are matched with similar policy instruments.

What is not the same, however, are the domestic structures - formal-institutional as well as informal-habitual - with which the demands and the instruments for their satisfaction are channeled and legitimized. In the first place, such notions as "middle class" demands are in themselves different in different societies.   The meaning of "middle class" values is not compre-hensible apart from other values and traditions that could be summarized as "political culture" and "economic-sociological culture."   It is surprising, in fact, that the concept of "economic culture" has not gained the same prominence as that accorded to "political culture." On a less abstract level, there is a good deal of dissimilarity in the domestic structures - formal-institutional as well as informal-habitual - with which the demands and the instruments for their satisfaction are channeled and legitimized.   In particular, the division of labor between state and society, the mix between public, semi-public, and private structures, the relations between interest groups and bureaucracies, the redistributive use of tax policies - to mention just a few examples -are significantly different in different types of industrialized societies. The domestic, political, and economic structures of industrialized societies, as well as the values that sustain them and the processes that are channelled through them, are quite divergent.   These divergencies have a great impact on the type of policies that are pursued and, equally important, how they are implemented. (13)

COORDINATION OF POLICIES AND THE NATION-STATE

From the beginning of European integration and of the integrative features of the Atlantic alliance, two contradictory processes (at times of unequal intensity) have been visible: a process of divergence and a process of integration. These contradictory trends have been analyzed in a long series of academic publications. A review of this literature, as well as of the public debate about the issues themselves, need not detain us here. One might suggest, however, that the process of coordination of policies among nation-states in the European and Atlantic Communities occupy a middle ground between the tendencies toward divergence and the tendencies toward integration.   In addition, one might suggest a spectrum of policies and attitudes that goes from divergence to parallelism, to coordination, to integration - a spectrum that ranges from minimal cooperation (divergence) to maximal institutional collaboration (integration).   All members of the European and Atlantic Communities have at different times, for different reasons, and on different issues pursued all four categories of policies. One could cite a number of well-known examples of policy divergencies as well as of integrative processes that have characterized transatlantic as well as intra-European political, economic, and strategic processes: de Gaulle's decision to remove France from the unified command structure of NATO (as well as other Gaullist foreign policy projects) would be an example of policy divergence; whereas the decisions to establish structures for a European Community in the form of the European Coal and Steel Community (ECSC), the European Economic Community (EEC), and the European Atomic Community (EURATOM), (within which conflicting national interests would be adjusted) would be an example of an integrative type of policy.

Located as they are at the two extremes of the divergence-parallelism-coordination-integration spectrum, such examples tend to be the most dramatic. It seems to me, however, that the more salient and timely issues in transatlantic and intra-European processes are located in the middle ground of the spectrum, in the areas of parallelism and coordination.

There is no question that in many important respects the political systems of Western Europe have become more and more alike. Although advanced industrialized societies share many characteristics, these parallelisms have not impelled them toward the establishment of more integrative structures but, at best, toward efforts to seek a better coordination of national policies. In other words, the parallelism resulting from the inherent dynamics of a consumer-oriented advanced industrial society need not, and in fact do not, lead to the intensification of integrative ventures. This is so not only because of internal domestic preoccupations but also because the members of the European Community have distinctly different bilateral interest relationships with their transatlantic partner, the United States.

At the same time there exists the inescapable logic, described in the earlier part of this paper, which propels governments to employ horizontal and to encourage lateral transactions in order to satisfy the internal-vertical demands pressed upon them by their electorates, which can be ignored only at the risk of being removed from office. It is primarily for this reason that the coordination of policies has become the central issue in intra-European as well as transatlantic relationships. Parallelism - the similarity of domestic developments, problems and demands - requires some form and measure of international and trans-national cooperation. But since the intensification of integrative processes is unacceptable to many members of the European Community for a variety of reasons, coordination appears to be the only acceptable alternative. In short, policy coordination has become a substitute for integration.

With the likelihood of an enlarged community emerging in the next few years, the prospects for intensified supra-national-integrative developments appear even more remote than they are at present. There is a question right now whether there are compelling inherent economic and monetary dynamics that require additional efforts toward integrative structures, or whether it is sufficient to solidify and streamline them. As Leon Lindberg and Stuart

Scheingold pointed out several years ago, important industrial and commercial interests in the Community appear to be interested primarily in conserving and substaining the present level of integration. They see their interests adequately served by the status quo and shy away from the uncertainties and readjustments which attend changes in the scope and intensity of supra-national arrangements. (14) Solidification and rationalization rather than intensification is the key phrase here, and the trend is as pronounced now as when Lindberg and Scheingold first described it. The "expansive logic of sector integration," as Ernst Haas called it, seems to have turned into the "status quo logic of sector integration," a logic which accepts and welcomes existing integrative structures but does not feel compelled to go beyond them, and which turns to coordination for problem-solving in novel situations.

A related consideration pertains to some rather technical monetary and commercial transactions. A decade ago Lawrence Krause noted a phenomenon even more pronounced now than it was then, that has contributed (along with other important factors) to the demise of a monetary union within the Community: "Governments do not need to be told . . . that excessive inflation in an open economy quickly leads to difficulties for themselves and their trading partners. They can see for themselves the rapidly deteriorating balance of payments, and pressures immediately arise for corrective actions. A 'hidden hand' toward policy coordination is directed by the market mechanism and it has proven to be very effective with the EEC." (15) Leaving the joint-floated currency snake (as an "integrative" device) toward the coordinating aspects of hammering out monetary assistance measures among the Community members is a typical example from the more recent past.

The possibilities for coordination in the area of indivisible goods, such as security issues and high politics foreign policy issues, are uneven and the record is mixed. The Western response to the issues presented by the European Security Conference was fairly well coordinated, but this was so in large part because West Germany's Ostpolitik and the resulting treaty arrangements had pre-empted and defused some major problem areas that were of vital concern to the Soviet Union and Eastern Europe. A coordinated European foreign policy program is as remote now as it has ever been. Barring major external shocks, which are unlikely to come from either the United States or the Soviet Union, there seems no compelling logic that would push the Comunity in that direction, especially in a decade in which governments are less inclined to pursue grandiose schemes for global and regional power rearrangements than, say, in the 1960s. (16)

Coordination on security issues is a special, and highly instructive example, for here one must distinguish between security as an end - which may be an indivisible product for an alliance as well as for a nation-state - and the means with which that end is achieved, for example through weapons procurement - which is of course a highly divisible commodity. Whether security is an indivisible product of the Western alliance, and of its regional European NATO component, is an issue that has plagued NATO for almost two decades. With the institutionalization of mutual assured destruction and "parity" in the SALT accords, Washington's European NATO partners (and especially the Federal Republic of Germany) can hardly feel reassured about the willingness of the United States to engage in strategic nuclear war in case of aggression through conventional means. If it were not for the fact that such an aggression appears highly unlikely, the fissures within NATO would be wider and deeper than they are. As it is, the issue has been swept under the rug, and when it tends to reappear in the open (for example, when Evans and Novak published leaked portions of the PRM-10 security study in August 1977) the rug is simply moved to cover it up again. With respect to the "indivisibility" of regional defense, the recent changes of the French military posture, as exemplified in the ideas of French Chief of Staff, General Guy Méry, appear somewhat more encouraging. (17) In either case (the transatlantic and the regional European), coordination of contingency planning has been employed to contain divergent tendencies, as exemplified in NATO's Eurogroup, the Western European Union and, to some extent, the Political Cooperation devices of the Community. With respect to the European regional context, this again provides an interesting contrast with the early 1950s when integrative rather than coordinating arrangements were envisaged, such as the plans for a European Defense Community. It should also be noted, however, that when indivisible security aspects, in which alliance members share equally, turn into divisible ones - for example, weapons procurement, weapons standardization, cost-sharing arrangements - coordination becomes much more difficult. In large part this is because of the mix between indivisible and divisible, ends-and-means aspects that characterize security issues. (18) Similar obstacles to coordination exist in energy policy and raw materials policy (19) because high politics tend to mingle with low politics, along the lines I have sought to redefine in the earlier part of this paper.

The opportunities and problems that shape the possibilities of coordination are, in important measure, connected with national divergencies of policy processes. This point has been made persuasively in several recent analyses. Peter Katzenstein has demonstrated, for example, how the differing relationships between state and society (as well as other related factors) in the United States and France have a profound impact on the success of coordinating economic and monetary policies. "The similarity in the policy networks linking state and society will determine the degree of similarity in government responses to problems of the international economy. The joint impact of international effects and domestic structures thus condition government policy .... Consistency and content of policies ... are the two primary dimensions which affect the coordination of policies between states .... (In) the French-American case government policies diverged along both dimensions, thus raising the greatest problems for the coordination of policies. The corporatist policy networks in the Federal Republic, to take another example, generate a foreign economic policy which is reminiscent of French policy in its great consistency but resembles American policy in its economic content. Policy coordination between West Germany and France as well as West Germany and the United States has, therefore, been more successful than between France and the United States." (20)

NATIONALISM AND INTERDEPENDENCE

The processes I have described in the preceding pages reflect a dialectic of interdependence and national interest calculations. Interest calculations by governments and sub-governmental groups, by society as well as by the state, have brought about interdependence and are compelled to operate within the range of opportunities and strictures which it exhibits. The processes of interdependence, in turn, are sustained by the policy consequences of these interest calculations which do not allow the disintegration of interdependence (toward a more fragmented, conflict-laden, non-coordinated system) but neither do they propel it toward further integration (toward institutional arrangements characterized by supra-national organizing principles). Interdependence, and the coordinating features required for its continued operation, is a half-way house between disintegration and integration of political and economic demand flows.

It needs to be stressed again, however, that the terminology of "national interest" in this context is not only ambiguous but misleading. Distributive value allocations, which have become the bulk of interdependence processes, are not shared equally (or, for that matter, equitably) by all segments of society, as would be those of a non-distributive nature such as security. It would seem to follow that a concept such as "nationalism," which derives its meaning from an undifferentiated view of the nation-state, seeing it as an organic whole and therefore permeated by non-distributive impulses, is essentially inappropriate for describing the central motivating forces that underlie most of the policy processes in the industrialized world. If we cannot even properly apply the term "national interest," with its rationalistic overtones, it would appear to be even more misleading to use the term "nationalism," with its emotive, irrational, and atavistic implications - implications that correspond much more to the nation-state concept that John Herz has seen as being eroded by various permeative processes. The concept of "nationalism" is analytically outdated, focusing as it does on an irrelevant view of territoriality and carrying with it the assumption that the nation, incorporated by its people, represents an undifferentiated whole and an undifferentiated sense of a common destiny. In short, the terminology of "nationalism" is inappropriate precisely because it is based primarily on the notion of indivisible values and the corresponding idea of high politics, at a time when most day-to-day political and economic processes are of the divisible kind.

I am aware of the paradox of having stated in the early part of this paper that "Nationalism is alive and well," and of now suggesting the inapplicability of the term itself. But this is not really as paradoxical as it seems. For one, there are still powerful emotive forces that focus on the nation as a communal organization which elicits feelings of identification and hence enlarges and enriches the meaning of public life. This cultural and sociological nationalism should perhaps be viewed as an understandable quest for a sense of continuity and meaning in a world that is undergoing rapid and fundamental changes which call into doubt traditional values and narrow the possibilities for personal commitment to, and self-identification with, a larger purpose. The secularization of both theological and political ideologies brings with it an agnostic pragmatism from which it is difficult to distill more than a consumption-oriented view of public life and a primitive utilitarianism that seeks to enhance pleasure and to avoid pain.   How such feelings of alienation find outlets in the self-identification with the outcome of international competitions - in sports as well as in other activities - is well-documented in sociological literature.

The political and economic-monetary processes of interdependence also narrow the possibilities for national self-identification, rendering its meaning more ambiguous and at times even contradictory, precisely because the interest calculations expressed in these processes cannot be unequivocally defined in national terms. In part they continue to be national, but they are at the same time larger and smaller - global as well as regional, provincial (in both senses of the term) as well as municipal. The domestic-national political system, the social and cultural environment within which most citizens have defined their well-being - spiritual as well as material - has by itself become deficient in providing that well-being - at the very least in its material sense, but most likely in a spiritual sense as well. This is, so-to-speak, the common human-political condition. Governments, in seeking to meet the demands pressed upon them by their electorates, are compelled to turn to external sources in order to meet these demands. But their reluctance to commit themselves totally either to divergence or to supra-national integration places them in an area of ambiguity where coordination appears as the reasonable as well as the necessary course of action. Yet the obstacles to coordination seem to arise from the differences among European states, although the needs that coordination is intended to meet seem to be common and widely shared.   Similar maladies are being addressed by dissimilar remedies. One is reminded of the controversy in the medical profession around the turn of the century between the proponents of "symptomatic" treatment and those who advocated treatment of the "cause." Europe, it seems to me, is too old a patient to be the subject of this kind of experimentation.

NOTES

(1)   John Lewis Gaddis, "Containment: A Reassessment," Foreign Affairs, July 1977, p. 885

(2)   John H. Herz, "The Rise and Demise of the Territorial State," World Politics, July 1957, pp. 473-93. Also see his International Politics in the Atomic Age (New York: Columbia University Press, 1959); see also Wolfram F. Hanrieder, "Compatibility and Consensus: A proposal for the Conceptual Linkage of External and Internal Dimensions of Foreign Policy," American Political Science Review, December 1967, pp. 971-82.

(3)   Daniel Bell, "The Future World Disorder: The Structural Context of Crises," Foreign Policy, Summer 1977, pp. 109-135, passim.

(4)   Richard Rosecrance and Arthur Stein, "Interdependence: Myth or Reality?" World Politics, October 1973, pp. 1-27. The quotations appear on p. 21 and p. 5, respectively. (Emphasis in original.)

(5) E.E. Schattschneider, The Semi-Sovereign People (New York: Holt, Rinehart and Winston, 1964), p.2

(6) For theoretical treatments of that issue, see Wolfram F. Hanrieder (ed.), Comparative Foreign Policy: Theoretical Essays (New York: David McKay, 1971).

(7) Karl Kaiser, "The U.S. and the EEC in the Atlantic System: The Problem of Theory," Journal of Common Market Studies, June 1967, pp. 338-435.

(8) See Robert Gilpin, "Three Models of the Future," in International Organization, Winter 1975, pp. 37-60. His third model, that of a neo-Mercantilist order, is especially pertinent to my argument.

(9) See the excellent review article by R. Harrison Wagner in International Organization, Summer 1974, pp. 435-466, which is entitled "Dissolving the State: Three Recent Perspectives on International Relations."

(10) See Norman Frohlich, Joe A. Oppenheimer, and Oran R. Young, Political Leadership and Collective Goods (Princeton, N.J.: Princeton University Press, 1971); and Norman Frohlich and Joe A. Oppenheimer, "Entrepreneurial Politics and Foreign Policy," World Politics, Spring 1972, pp. 151-78.

(11) See, for example, Gerard Chaliand, Revolution in the Third World (New York: Viking, 1977).

(12) Bell, op. cit.

(13) See, for example, Peter J. Katzenstein, "International Relations and Domestic Structures: Foreign Economic Policies of Advanced Industrial States," International Organization, Winter 1976, pp. 1-45; Henrik Schmiegelow and Michele Schmiegelow, "The New Mercantilism in International Relations: The Case of France's External Monetary Policy," International Organization, Spring 1975, pp. 367-391; Isaiah Frank and Ryokichi Hirono, eds., How the United States and Japan See Each Other's Economy: An Exchange of Views Between the American and Japanese Committees for Economic Development (New York: Committee for Economic Development, 1974); Edward L. Morse, Modernization and the Transformation of International Relations (New York: Free Press, 1976); Arnold J. Heidenheimer, Hugh Heclo, and Carolyn Teich Adams, Comparative Public Policy: The Politics of Social Choice in Europe and America (New York: St. Martin's Press, 1976); Jack Hayward and Michael Watson, eds., Planning, Politics and Public Policy: The British, French, and Italian Experience (New York: Cambridge University Press, 1975); Helen Wallace, William Wallace and Carole Webb, eds., Policy-Making in the European Communities (New York: John Wiley & Sons, 1977).

(14) Leon N. Lindberg and Stuart A. Scheingold, Europe's Would-be Polity (Englewood Cliffs, N.J.: Prentice-Hall, 1970); also see Philippe C. Schmitter, "A Revised Theory of Regional Integration," in Leon N. Lindberg and Stuart A. Scheingold, eds. Regional Integration, Theory and Research (Cambridge, Mass.: Harvard University Press, 1971), pp. 232-264.

(15) For an elaboration of this argument, see Roger D. Hansen, "European Integration: Forward March, Parade Rest, or Dismissed?" International Organization, Spring 1973, pp. 225-254. The quotation from Krause appears in fn. 21, p. 231.

(16) Cf. Stanley Hoffmann, "Toward a Common European Foreign Policy?", in Wolfram F. Hanrieder, ed., The United States and Western Europe: Political, Economic and Strategic Perspectives (Cambridge, Mass.: Winthrop Publishers, 1974), pp. 79-105; also see Stanley Hoffmann, "Obstinate or Obsolete? The Fate of the Nation-State and the Case of Western Europe," Daedalus, Summer 1966, pp. 862-915.

(17) See Strategic Survey, 1976 (London, IISS, 1976), pp. 66-71.

(18) See Mancur Olson, Jr., The Logic of Collective Action: Public Goods and the Theory of Groups (Cambridge, Mass.: Harvard University Press, 1965); James Buchanan, The Demand and Supply of Public Goods (Chicago: Rand McNally, 1968).

(19) See Werner J. Feld, "Atlantic Interdependence and Competition for Raw Materials in the Third World," Atlantic Community Quarterly, Fall 1976, pp. 369-377.

(20) Katzenstein, op. cit., p. 19 and p. 44; also see William Wallace, "Issue Linkage Among Atlantic Governments," International Affairs, April 1976, pp. 163-179; Stephen D. Krasner, "Are Bureaucracies Important?," Foreign Policy, Summer 1972, pp. 159-79; and H. Schmiegelow and M. Schmiegelow, op. cit.

5 Reflections on the Papers by Professors Northedge and Hanrieder
E. O. Czempiel

The two papers offer a new proof for the fact, not unknown in the social sciences, that you can start from totally different points of view and come to the same conclusions. F.S. Northedge has drawn heavily on the history of American-European relations and has given many interesting and stimulating insights into the turning point of this history. There are many facts with which most of us will agree, and there are solid arguments for his thesis that there is a New Nationalism within the Atlantic region and that its causes are to be found in the increased concern with economic achievement and welfare. Wolfram Hanrieder starts from a very elaborated and highly abstract model of foreign policy-making within an international environment, and his conclusion is remarkably similar. The vitality of the nation-state stems from the fact that distributive matters have become more important than the non-distributive ones; welfare and economic issues have become more important than the issue of defense. The New Nationalism has its roots in the risen expectations of economic well-being in the Western states.

If two distinguished authors reach the same conclusion, nobody likes to disagree. However, it is difficult to accept the conclusion that the dividing factor within the Atlantic Community is the well-being of the people. Does not, on the contrary, this economic well-being demand closer cooperation between the Western states? Is not interdependence, as a term and a situation, (1) valid particularly for the field of economics? F.S. Northedge gives the answer: It is true, but only in theory, not in practice. There is a difference between the "logic of cooperation," established by liberal theory and the brutal facts of economic decision-making in modern states. Decisions have to be made in order to satisfy short-run economic demands, to allocate specific and visible values. International cooperation only makes sense if a large share of it benefits the national allocation. Deficits in the balance of payments and scarcity of resources both lead to complications, not to cooperation. The crucial question is not concerned with the degree of interdependence, but "How many Concordes have been sold this year?" This concern for economic gains, says Northedge, has coincided with the coming of detente in East-West relationships. The common interest in defense has given way to the unilateral interest in economic gains. The Atlantic Community in defense matters has been weakened by the economic nationalism of the Atlantic nations.

Hanrieder offers, in effect, a similar argument. Defense is a non-distributive, non-divisible issue while economics and welfare have a distributive-divisible character. Since detente has weakened these non-distributive and non-divisible elements in the Atlantic Community, the distributive-divisible issues have become more and more important. Because of the liberal, integrative character of the international system, these types of decisions tend to dominate the vertical (domestic) field as well as the horizontal (international) field. (2) Summing up (and simplifying somewhat): both authors argue that the danger for the Atlantic Community stems from the growing importance of economic and social matters.

It is not this conclusion, but its possible consequences which might be disturbing. Is the Atlantic Community up to an alternative between cooperation and economic progress? Must we abandon one in order not to lose the other? Do we depend on a high degree of tension in order to preserve the coherence of the Western nations? Within NATO there is a certain tendency to answer in the positive, to step up armaments and military cooperation not only to deter the Russians, but also to stabilize the degree of cooperation between the Western states. There is a tendency to mobilize support by pointing again to the military danger coming from augmented Russian armaments. Obviously, Atlantic coherence and a stable amount of military spending are interconnected. To put it differently, there is a negative relationship between detente and the degree of cooperation between the Atlantic nations.

In addition to the explanations given by the two authors, there is perhaps a third one. What we call New Nationalism is not an original phenomenon. It is, on the contrary, only the reflex of the fact that we do not have a political concept of cooperation. We never had one. The West has had a concept of military cooperation in the tradition of European military alliances. Everybody was quickly and profoundly convinced that the danger from the Soviet Union could be faced only by military cooperation. Only a few people realize that cooperation in the field of economics and social welfare are equally important for security.

Security has been interpreted in a traditional old-fashioned way as military security. But this is only one aspect, an important one, but not the only one. When the Cold War started, the West was very well aware that the basic conflict with the East was not a military but a political and social one. At stake is the system of government within liberal democracy and liberal society. In this realm security means to conserve democracy by stabilizing the consensus for this type of government. We should remind ourselves that Portugal was one of the staunchest members of the Atlantic Alliance. There was, nevertheless, a good chance that she would turn communist, and the chance is still there. Security means primarily to have a solid consensus for liberal democracy. This consensus depends on an accepted distribution of economic and political values. Jean-Baptiste Say (1767-1832) argued that the best defense against enemies is a high degree of economic and social consensus. This is all the more important in our day when the mass media and much better education have increased the expectations of all.

It is certainly not easy to learn that economic problems such as unemployment, inflation, and exchange rate troubles cannot be solved unilaterally. Usually political leaders have no education in economics; they have difficulty understanding what is going on. Economists themselves find it is not easy to interpret the situation. Even if the knowledge needed to solve the problems exists, it is extremely difficult to reach common decisions. The quarrel between the United States and the Federal Republic of Germany over fiscal policies in the spring of 1978 is a case in point.

There is a third aspect, however. Economic concepts are very much influenced by economic interests. Usually it is the middle and the upper classes who define these concepts and these interests. At the same time, these classes are not very much affected by problems such as inflation, unemployment, and the general deterioration of Lebensqualität. On the contrary, during the 30 years of Cold War orientation they have made themselves at home with a system of value distribution which was oriented toward a military defined concept of security. At the same time it is this two-fifths of a nation which is usually interested in foreign policy (3) with the vast majority of the population being much too occupied with the problem of making a living.

If this reasoning is valid, what we need most is a new concept of foreign policy. Both authors have touched this task; Wolfram Hanrieder has tackled it at some length. Both authors, in my view, have left out completely the social dimension which a new concept of foreign policy certainly must consider. Let me give one example: the AFL-CIO traditionally has been one of the greatest supporters of military and political cooperation between the United States and the Western European countries. It is one of the most outspoken critics of a simple interpretation of detente. (4) On the other hand, American workers suffer considerably from inflation and unemployment and from the investment policies of the multi-national corporations.(5) Without acknowledging, or seeing, the contradiction with its political position, the AFL-CIO has asked for protective politics in trade matters. (6) It is completely entitled to do so as long as political cooperation is not coupled with the respective economic cooperation. Employment must be shared in the same way as military security; inflation must not be exported, but must be dealt with cooperatively in order to distribute damages and benefits for all concerned.

I would like to underline the point both authors have made against foreign policy as a field separate from politics. It seems to me, however, that we must go further than that. Politics is, and always has been, distribution of values. It is more or less unimportant whether these values are domestic or non-domestic by origin. There is, in fact, no difference between certain environments within which the allocation of values takes place. (7) What we need is a concept of policy-making which is comprehensive in this regard and comprehensive also in regard to economic and political values for all social strata. Such a concept will bridge the gap between liberal theory and political practice, since it will demonstrate that what is blocking the realization of the liberal concept is not a historical necessity but a social constellation. It will demonstrate above all that it is impossible to cooperate militarily and to compete economically and socially. It will evidence the inter-relatedness between the military and the economic content of security and will give priority to the latter.

What is needed most, therefore, is this comprehensive concept of politics within a region such as the Western states, although, properly speaking, this is really not a region. Disregarding the geographical aspect, there is, above all, an asymmetry between the United States and the small European states. The term "region" points only toward the fact that all the Western states have much in common, that there is interdependence as well as independence. There is also the particular interrelationship between the member states of the European Community with its uncertain and undefined future. However, all have a common basis in liberalism, democratic government, social justice, and freedom. This is what has been called the "Euro-American System." (8) The processes within this system need to be guided by a complex of adequate political concepts.

It is rather easy to see that such concepts depend very much on a theoretical analysis and explanation of these processes. The political concepts, the concepts of politicians, need guidance from the academic community. It is not sufficient for political science to point toward a phenomenon and give it a new name. What is needed is a theoretically guided explanation which provokes adequate political concepts. This new concept will be needed not only to explain the New Nationalism but also to get rid of it.

NOTES

(1) For discussion of the term "Interdependence" from a German point of view, see Manfred Knapp: "Politische und wirtschaftliche Interdependenzen im Verhaltnis USA-(Bundesrepublik) Deutschland 1945-1975" in: M. Knapp, W. Link, et al. (eds.) Die USA und Deutschland 1918-1975 (Munchen 1978).

(2) It is not clear whether Hanrieder uses the term "Re-distribution" in the same sense as Theodore J. Lowi. See his "American Business, Public Policy: Case-studies and Political Theory," in World Politics, 16, 4, July 1964, pp. 677 ff.

(3) For the relation between education and attention, see William Schneider, "Public Opinion: The Beginning of Ideology?" in Foreign Policy 17, Winter 1974-75, pp. 88 ff.

(4) Philip Taft, Defending Freedom, American Labor and Foreign Affairs (Los Angeles: Nash Publishing, 1973). For a very new and interesting analysis of the foreign policy of American trade unions see Werner Link, Deutsche und amerikanische Gewerkschaften und Geschaftsleute 1945-1975. Eine Studie uber transnationale Beziehungen, Dusseldorf: Droste Verlag, 1978.

(5) See statement of George Meany, in United States Congress, 94/1 and 2, Committee on Foreign Relations, Senate: Foreign Policy Choices for the seventieth and eightieth, Hearings, Vol. 1, Washington 1976, p. 194 ff. 206 ff.

(6) See the Burke-Hartke Bill in trade matters, 1974.

(7)   I have elaborated on this problem in my book on American foreign policy, forthcoming.

(8)   This has been the subject of an international conference, the results of which have been published by E.O. Czempiel and Dankwart Rustow (eds.), The Euro-American System (Frankfurt: Campus Verlag; and Boulder, Colorado: Westview Press, 1976).

6 The New Economic Nationalism and the Coordination of Economic Policies
Edward L. Morse

The recession of the mid-1970s may be debated with respect to its origins, its significance as a turning-point in post-World War II history, or its theoretical and practical lessons for scholars and members of the policy community. Nonetheless, it demonstrates clearly a dilemma at the center of global politics today. Economic production and distribution have become internationalized and in that process of internationalization they have become more important political factors in the complex equations that define governmental authority and legitimacy. Since there are insufficient mechanisms to control these international economic processes, individual governments, in their efforts to protect themselves against threats to their integrity, rely primarily upon the most secure framework for control - national autonomy. The contradiction between the international integrative processes of economic growth and the fragmentation of the international policy into some 150 sovereign communities poses problems that no government can escape. And, like the familiar prisoner in his oft-cited quandary, governments, acting typically to preserve their acquired economic gains, pursue economic policies from which other societies - and their own as well - suffer severe consequences.

This is, in short, the New Economic Nationalism. Unlike the economic nationalism of List's Germany, Hamilton's America, or Tojo's Japan, the principal aims of today's economic nationalism are not to increase one state's power or wealth at the expense of others, or to secure permanent national gains through territorial expansion or hegemonial control. Today's economic nationalism is not motivated by, nor does it thrive in, a climate of interstate competition which, like the classical balance of power, postulates a world of political finiteness, physical insecurity, and bellicosity. Its motivations are far more complex, obviously depending upon such contextual circumstances as national resource endowment, level of economic development, and legitimacy of governmental institutions. In spite of these complexities, it is clear that economic nationalism today is motivated, wherever it appears, by the fear of economic vulnerability to processes that

66

are poorly understood and lie outside a government's control. It is motivated by the apprehension that unless certain actions are taken - the imposition of quotas, the use of export subsidies, and the protection of high technology sectors - a government will lose power to opposition forces at home because of its failure to cope with unemployment or, in a longer run, will relinquish the opportunity to provide the basis for national advancement. It is further motivated by the desire to control one's own national patrimony, lest owners of capital or technology from abroad receive an unjust share of one's own wealth and, through that capital or technology, an undue say over one's national political fate.

The New Economic Nationalism is born from fear rather than opportunity, although in practice it might appear indistinguishable from the latter. As Pierre Hassner has argued,

> The real race may be less to increase one's comparative power than to decrease one's comparative vulnerability, to manipulate not only an opponent's weaknesses, but one's own, to encourage exported erosion or to control contagious explosions, to modify or maintain not so much territorial borders or even diplomatic alignments as what might be called the balance of wills and the balance of expectations. (1)

Its manifestation is different, depending upon whether it appears in the United States or Mexico, France or the Federal Republic of Germany, Hungary or Brazil. Wherever it appears, it contradicts the argument that international economic interdependence constrains governments to use cooperative economic strategies and to avoid conflictual ones. (2) Yet its radical differences from the motivations of what might be called classical economic nationalism make cooperative patterns not only plausible, but likely.

This is not the place to repeat at length arguments I and others have put forward concerning the multiple relationships between the processes of modernization, the growth in international interdependence, and changes in the substance of procedures of foreign economic policy. (3) Nor still do I wish to make hair-splitting distinctions between what is old and new about economic nationalism in determining, for example, whether the governments of Iran or Brazil today resemble more closely the United States of the 1970s or Germany of the 1870s in the way they conduct foreign economic policy. My aim is narrower.

I wish to sketch out some of the factors that seem to underlie this New Economic Nationalism. The factors upon which I will focus in this essay are by no means exhaustive. Nor, except at a very general level, will I try to typologize different policies in terms of the kinds of societies with which they tend to be associated. The general distinction involves relatively modernized as opposed to relatively non-modernized societies. Other useful distinctions include level of openness and size of the economy including resource endowment. One other potentially useful distinction is type of political regime - whether we are dealing with a command economy system or a market-based system, a centralized or federal structure, an elected government or some other form of government. This last distinction must be used cautiously. Hungary's government, like the United States', pursues an economic policy aimed at the development of a universal, non-discriminatory MFN (Most Favored Nation) system of commercial relations, yet one could scarcely attribute this similarity in policy to the type of political regime each society has.

ECONOMIC NATIONALISM IN THE ADVANCED INDUSTRIAL SOCIETIES

For complex reasons, most of which are beyond the scope of the argument in this essay, the foreign policies of highly industrialized societies have focused more intensively on economic objectives than on more traditional objectives relating to the territorial integrity of the state. (4) Governments in pluralistic as well as authoritarian states find their authority and legitimacy based upon their ability to deliver jobs, maintain relatively stable prices, distribute wealth equitably, enlarge the economic pie, and provide a better quality of life. This has not meant that all security dilemmas have become resolved, that the fascination of governments or pressure groups with high technology aims has become muted, or that the perennial attraction for transcendental goals like power or national glory have disappeared. But these latter, more traditional foreign policy objectives now compete with the newer ones, and the balance struck within any one society will virtually always have to include a rather significant dose of economic welfare goals.

Several complicating factors should be borne in mind before we explore somewhat further the basis of the New Economic Nationalism in the industrialized world. First, these new economic welfare goals are generally oriented inwardly rather than outwardly. Since governments are valued by their citizens to the degree that they are able to provide a better life, and since, especially in democratic systems, governments will likely lose power and authority if they cannot satisfy citizens' expectations, economic welfare (which I am using as a short-hand expression for the objectives listed above) infuses national political life. (5) Second, at the same time - and probably for the same reasons - that these economically based objectives became salient or politicized, the industrial world witnessed an extraordinary growth in international interdependence. Among the features of this more systemic phenomenon are the following: national economic goals can now be significantly enhanced by diverse forms of cooperative relations among governments; national governments have become more vulnerable and sensitive to policies pursued by those same governments with which they would likely want to cooperate; multiple and complex linkages among societies have meant that national strategies have to be carried out with multiple partners on multiple chess boards, with the ever-present danger that mutual vulnerabilities will be translated into permanent paralysis; and, in the midst of a new and complex cooperative environment, new opportunities have arisen for complex forms of nationalism. (6) This new mercantalism is similar to the old in that one party can gain more than others; but, unlike the old, these gains can take place in a world which is not beggar-thy-neighbor, for all parties can gain something.

The general point to be made is that foreign economic policies in the industrial world are complex, mixed-motive phenomena. They are simultaneously cooperative and conflictual, and in most instances the incentives for cooperation or conflict are rooted in internal domestic political processes. Most of the argument below concentrates on processes and factors that lead toward the adoption of competive or conflictual policies. It should be borne in mind that these policies are only part of the story and that this essay is not addressed to the examination of the balance between the two types of orientation.

Several factors feed into the New Economic Nationalism. Since the onset of stagflation in the 1970s, these factors appear to represent a trend that is to continue ineluctably over the next decade or so. Whether this is the case is an open question.

One factor, which seems to be paramount, stems from the political consequences of the growth in international interdependence. (7) The increased sensitivity of economics that have become interdependent represents a loss of control by governments over their economies. The growth in interdependence increases the number of unknown factors that governments try to take into account in implementing short-range as well as longer-range policies. This is another way of saying that interdependence serves to reduce the number of policy instruments available to achieve different objectives. In this sense, economic nationalism results from attempts by governments to create new policy instruments that are designed either to achieve positive goals - higher growth rates, fuller employment - or, as is more often the case, to reduce the vulnerability of society to activities originating abroad. Thus, the New Economic Nationalism aims less at the achievement of external policy goals, less at the attainment of international economic power, and more at creating a buffer against imported crises - imported inflation or recession, imported loss of control.

Needless to say, its effects can be the same as those of a more positive economic nationalism - exported crises, exported inflation or recession, and exported vulnerability or loss of control. At the present time, an immediate worry is that the accumulative effects of such policies as export subsidies to enhance employment will be the complete unraveling of the already highly comprised rules of liberal trade.

There is, to be sure, a degree of faddishness in this analysis. So long as interdependence was accompanied by almost 20 years of uninterrupted growth in the industrial world after World War II, it was highly valued and the norms that developed to regulate it in commercial and monetary matters were by and large honored. After the energy crisis of 1973-74, the initial quadrupling of oil prices, and the synchronization of short-term economic cycles in the industrialized world (East as well as West) interdependence, in terms of recession and inflation became recognized for what it had always been: a Damocles sword providing both the possibilities for unprecedented gains far larger than any government could achieve for its society on its own, and a source of vulnerability to foreign disruptions as well.

One result of this new perception is that like those earlier forms of economic nationalism at the end of the nineteenth century or during the

1930s, the new form raises doubts about the desirability or feasibility of a liberal system of world trade and payments based on market conditions. The principles of universal free trade and instrumental monetary mechanisms are soured all the more in that governments wish to take advantage of commercial and monetary instruments - in contravention to the norms of the GATT (General Agreement on Tariffs and Trade) or a liberal monetary system - as additional means to help them fulfill goals that are nationalistic in nature and that feed into a neo-merchantilist perspective: namely, that a government follows a policy which, all other things being equal, will benefit it at the expense of others.

The current situation provides multiple examples of this fear of the vulnerability of one society to others and of the reluctance of any single government to take policy actions to help others out of the recession. Even the stronger industrial societies of the West - the United States, Japan, and the Federal Republic of Germany - are, like the others, reluctant to incur trade deficits or to reduce enormous trade surpluses, which they would do if, through reflationary policies, they were to import more goods from the others, inducing export-led growth in the latter. However, the current situation should not obscure a more fundamental set of factors to which we will return. While interdependence can instill cooperative relations in periods of growth, it is a breeding ground of economic nationalism in periods of recession; the efficient and satisfactory management of interdependence requires that some governments be willing to incur risks or sacrifices in order to preserve or to create a more manageable and less conflictual system of relationships. (8)

Additional complications have developed in relations among industrial societies and in the policies pursued by many of their governments because of the internal mechanisms of what we might call, in short-hand terms, the welfare-state. As Jacques Pelkmans recently argued,

> Autonomy constitutes the basis for the political responsibility (especially of democratically elected political leaders), tied up with the guarantee of a considerable degree of discretionary spending. A substantial reduction of policy-autonomy is a threat to the welfare-state; it touches upon the assumed capacity to pursue policies, that is to sustain the fundamental commitment to voters. The lack of control over the outcome of market processes brings them to the mercy of international economic developments and this is precisely what the welfare-states do not wish. (9)

In welfare-states, in short, there is a dual propensity. On the one hand, there is a desire to increase market interdependence and policy interdependence with neighbors in order to maximize gains from trade and a larger effective tax base for redistributive policies. This has traditionally been a significant factor in each member of the European Community's quest for greater integration. If German society and business could gain from producing for a larger guaranteed market for German goods, Italy's could benefit from Community development projects in its backward south. On the other hand, there is in welfare-states also the desire to reduce both market interdependence and policy interdependence in order to restrict the consequences of government control over the domestic economy. Welfare states almost automatically create what Theodore Geiger has called the "neo-national rule of experts" who see their own fortunes and national autonomy as inextricably linked. (10)

The dualism and schizophrenia of the modern industrial state is, of course, accompanied by the ambivalence of what John Hicks called the "Administrative Revolution" of this century. As Hicks argued, during World War I, the Russian Revolution, and the Depression of the 1930s, governments "created new techniques and instruments of administration which could be used in a new way, for the attainment of social objectives - welfare - that had formerly been quite out of reach. But they could also be used in the old ways: for the regulation of trade, and economic activity generally, in the national interest." (11)

The dual aspects of the welfare-state know no easy resolution. They create an impulse toward contraction of interdependence which can reinforce political isolationism. They also push governments toward increased policy interdependence as a means of controlling the external environment, if other factors support such openness. However, a third policy choice exists: the mutual limitation of autonomy by all welfare-states. "The loyalty to cooperate is negative: welfare-states 'buy-off' some of the 'beggar-thy-neighbor' policies while leaving sufficient discretion, loopholes and escape clauses to have the conventions or treaties accepted at home." (12) I have looked at these choices elsewhere. (13) For the present purpose it is important to note that one of the continuing tendencies of welfare-states is the maintenance of control over the internal environment. Theodore Geiger describes a related factor as follows: "... during the past hundred years, Western societies, for the sake of democratic social-welfare values, have been reversing at a gradually accelerating pace the liberal state's earlier substitution of efficiency criteria for the aristocratic social values of the patrimonial order." (14)

No domestic goals - oriented toward services and the quality of life - are being pursued in industrialized societies, in part because of the growth in demand for these objectives by citizens and in part because of the tendencies of people, working in bureaucratic structures, to expand their own decision domains. These goals are in part distributive, and relate to the equitable distribution of income and greater economic security for groups who have not benefited fully from economic growth - the old, the sick, and the poor. The goals are also oriented toward quality-of-life services, including environmental quality, medical care, education, and police protection. Some societies have been able to manage this substitution of welfare criteria for efficiency criteria through an acceleration of economic productivity and international market integration. Others, especially the United States, have not. This situation is in part responsible for the deterioration in the ability of governments to assure the simultaneous achievement of the magic square of policy objectives - stable prices, full employment, balance of payments equilibrium, and economic growth. It is, therefore, also responsible for the imposition of governmental controls which interfere with market forces at micro-economic levels in domestic as well as in international markets. These models of interference frequently carry neo-mercantile tendencies.

Whether this general factor will, by itself, lead to a more economically nationalistic world is open to debate. Not all societies will follow the route of the United Kingdom. Sweden, for example, has until recently been able to pursue welfare goals without losing the gains for efficiency criteria. Even in the United Kingdom efforts to cope with this alleged dilemma of "post-industrial" society will continue in what is now an experimental laboratory for the rest of the industrial world. However, until this dilemma is resolved it poses problems for industrial societies everywhere and for the management of relations among them.

A fourth set of factors has rather inadvertently fed into the process of economic nationalism. It is a complex set of factors, which should be spelled out in some detail concerning the difficulties governments have confronted in maintaining neutral monetary mechanisms in their international economic relationships. The establishment of such neutral mechanisms as universal media to carry out economic transactions (dollars, gold, Special Drawing Rights) and the restriction of the uses of these mechanisms is a centerpiece of liberal trade and payments rules established at Bretton Woods. Without going into the details of why this is the case, neutral monetary instruments are designed to impede international economic conflicts and to foster economic cooperation among governments. They have, however, increasingly failed to serve cooperative ends, largely because of the growth in burdens that governments have imposed upon monetary instruments. This growth occurred in both international and domestic realms.

Internationally, the monetary mechanism did not simply have a passive role in defusing the politicization of adjustment or of assuring growth in international market competitiveness. Even if it had been restricted to these purposes, it would have created difficulties. Adjustment had become a sticky political issue not only because parity changes became especially charged before 1971, but also because adjustment was hampered by other governmental policies designed to meet other national goals - full employment, or the maintenance of industries with declining comparative advantages for over-riding national purposes. Market competitiveness was undermined by the growth in trade of goods and services which, to one degree or another, were associated with enterprises exempt from the rules of an ideal market system - agriculture, monopolistic enterprises especially in areas of high technology, and some nationalized industries.

Additionally, however, monetary mechanisms grew to have other uses, some of which were directly redistributive and others of which were perceived as being redistributive. These redistributive aspects of international monetary mechanisms inevitably challenged the de facto ability of the mechanisms to fulfill the more neutral regulatory roles they were predominately designed to play and made it appear, as in the case with all redistributive mechanisms, that some societies would gain unfairly at the expense of others. Thus, the provision of additional liquidity to bolster first sterling and then the dollar appeared to have this redistributive role - from poorer states to Britain and the United States. More recently, plans to link the creation of new liquidity to economic development had this role also - from OECD countries to developing countries.

When other uses and burdens of international monetary mechanisms are added to these it is clear that the more restricted and neutral uses to which monetary mechanisms were to be put overwhelmed the capacity of governments to maintain them. I have in mind such uses as controlling the extensive private financial markets and, especially, integrating the newly rich countries - both OPEC and other financial newcomers - into a managerial club whose members heretofore have been the original industrialized societies of the world.

Domestically, too, new burdens were placed on the monetary mechanisms. Neutral monetary mechanisms imply the use of two other general policy instruments for adjustment purposes: changes in the exchange rate and demand management. Harry Johnson has addressed himself to the latter:

> Demand management would consequently be the only problem for macroeconomic policy-making. Furthermore, with sufficient inter-national mobility of capital, demand-management boils down to fiscal policy, with monetary policy serving only the function of determining the level and rate of growth of the country's international reserves. (15)

However, this perspective on the domestic uses of monetary policy is rather unrealistic. As desirable as it might seem in some quarters to restrict the uses of monetary instruments in the management of the domestic economy and to subordinate them to fiscal instruments, this view is by no means universally accepted.

Monetary instruments have gained increasingly widespread use in the world for both short-term demand management purposes and for purposes of long-term structural planning. Whether or not desirable, this has been and is likely to continue to be the case. The efficacy of fiscal instruments depends upon national political characteristics which are by no means found universally in the world, or even held in common by industrialized societies. To the degree that fiscal instruments are not available, the mix of fiscal and monetary instruments will stress the latter. Moreover, the growth in the number and scope of governmental objectives in domestic matters - whether by reason of increased demands made by a politicized public, or by reason of the need for increased governmental interventions to manage a highly integrated national economy - has led governments to use whatever policy instruments they have available to them. This also has led to the multiple and frequently contradictory uses of monetary instruments to assure such objectives as stability of prices, full employment, balance of payments equilibrium, and long-term social and economic changes.

The upshot, again, is an overload on the internationl monetary regime. National monetary instruments, invoked for an increasing number of domestic goals, impede the maintenance of international monetary instruments to facilitate international commerce or ease balance-of-payment adjustments. In this sense, they reinforce the movement toward a New Economic Nationalism in the industrialized world.

Another set of factors in the New Economic Nationalism relates to the pursuit by governments of current account surpluses in their overall foreign policies.   Mercantalism has, in fact, been traditionally associated with current account surpluses.   But in classical mercantilism a surplus was pursued largely because of the belief that it brought accumulated wealth, in the form of gold or claims on other economies, into the coffers of a government. It has long been recognized that surpluses on trade in goods and services are irrational from the point of view of accumulated wealth. All other things being equal, surpluses involve the consumption by others of one's own national product and the consumption of less than an economy produces. From the point of view of accumulation of weath a more rational policy would involve the consistent pursuit of current account deficits.   This does not mean that surpluses do not involve gains for a society.   They can, depending on the conditions under which they are sought.   Whether rational or not, the pursuit of current account surpluses has become normalized throughout the industrial world. Like classical mercantilism, its new versions are conflictual insofar as not all governments can successfully pursue surpluses at once.   At least one economy must residually be in deficit since trade accounts inevitably sum to zero.   The reasons for the pursuit of surpluses have become increasingly varied. What follows is, therefore, little more than a checklist of the multiple incentives for seeking current account surpluses.

Full-employment and other macro-economic policy goals are central to any discussion of modern mercantilism.   The more open an economy and the more output and employment are related to world market conditions, the more likely will full-employment policies involve production in export industries.   While it may be doubtful that, as some left-wing economists argue, full-employment policies inevitably involve neo-mercantilist policies, it is clear that this is sometimes the case.   Joan Robinson put forward this argument in its most widely-discussed form as follows:

Ever since the war (World War II), partly by good luck, partly by good management and partly by the arms race, overall effective demand has been kept from serious relapses. Nowadays governments are conerned not just to maintain employment, but to make national income grow. Nevertheless, the capitalist world is still always somewhat of a buyer's market, in the sense that capacity to produce exceeds what can be sold at a profitable price... The chronic condition for industrial enterprise is to be looking around anxiously for industrial enterprise is to be looking round anxiously for prospects of sales. Since the total market does not grow fast enough to make room for all, each government feels it a worthy and commendable aim to increase its own share in world activity for the benefit of its own people.
This is the new merchantalism. (16)

No observer of the international economy today can miss the thrust of Professor Robinson's statement.   Even before the relapses in effective demand that accompanied the recent recession, it was obvious that some governments - most notably Japan - quite consciously pursued current account surpluses for essentially domestic demand management purposes or as part of a tacit social contract between business and labor. The recession of 1975-77 universalized the pressures on governments to foster exports as a means of maintaining or increasing employment at home, coupled, of course, with the perceived need to increase exports to offset oil imports. While stresses on the liberal trading system have been constrained in the short-run, prospects for avoiding protectionism - the other side of the coin of the drive to export - are not great.

In addition to ends served in demand management, other ends are served by the New Economic Nationalism. These include the political incentive to combat protectionism at home by fostering gains from trade and bolstering the interests of unions and businesses in the export sector. (17) There is also the desire to create markets abroad for home produced goods in order to assure the growth of certain industries, especially those related to high technology where research and development costs are high. (18) Governments in both middle-sized economies such as Japan, France, or Britain and in large economies such as the United States find it desirable to invest in advanced technology for many reasons, including national defense, fearing that to do otherwise would inhibit long-term economic growth, and the desire to maintain national autonomy. If investments in advanced technology are to prove economically feasible, markets far larger than those provided in the domestic sphere must be sought in order to maximize production and to lower costs. Thus in areas of advanced technology one also finds an incentive to achieve current account surpluses.

If the current account is divided into its major segments - trade and services - an additional motivation for the fostering of trade surpluses becomes apparent. Many governments, especially the Federal Republic of Germany, have tended to run continuous deficits on services. In the German case, service deficits include imports of military hardware, offset arrangements for American and other foreign troops stationed in Germany for purposes of national defense, tourism, and remittance abroad made principally by alien residents employed in national industry. Indeed, in this latter category, the importation of foreign workers, a variant of mercantilism has become significant in the modern world. Rather than export capital, some societies have found it desirable to import cheap foreign laborers who provide an additional benefit in that they are the first to be laid off in case of recession. However, the main point is that quasi-permanent deficits on services must be offset on the other side of the current account by means of trade surpluses.

An additional set of factors that carry neo-mercantilist implications relate to what Preeg calls the "conflict betwen the economic gains from trade and competing national objectives":

It reflects the growing economic role of governments in all industrialized countries... The policy objectives could include regional development, a higher degree of self-sufficiency for particular sectors of the economy - from agriculture to computers to fuels - or environmental standards. To some extent, these objectives are pursued through the use of protective tariffs but they are also affected by a variety of nontariff barriers from quotas to public financial support to preferential procurement policies. (19).

These issues of domestic legislation affecting international trade are so much a part of contemporary governance that many observers have called for a continuing process of international negotiation to avoid their detrimental concomitants.

Finally, there are more traditional and overtly mercantilist reasons for pursuing current account surpluses which relate to the desire of governments to finance other sorts of foreign activities. For most of the industrialized societies, a current account, or trade surplus, enables them to implement policies to aid the less-developed world. In the absence of a trade surplus, governments would find it economically and politically difficult to grant aid to less developed countries on a continuing basis or to foster trade imports from less developed countries. Surpluses also foster the growth of multinational direct investment abroad whether or not such investment is abetted by governments. In the case of the United States, external security and economic interests are also involved. Trade surpluses facilitate the financing of troops stationed abroad as well as the fighting of wars. There was, therefore, validity to the argument put forward by many Europeans in the late 1960s that they were helping to finance American participation in the war in Vietnam. A trade surplus for the United States was also seen as a requisite for world trade, a policy that also irked Europeans insofar as it meant continued American dominance in the international financial system.

A review of economic nationalism in the industrialized world should also take into account the political forces that are mobilized in a period of generalized recession. While these might not have the same historical force as the other factors put forward earlier, they have certainly, under present conditions, exacerbated countervailing internationalist forces that would lead to cooperative strategies. The tendency of governments to impose restrictions on imports or on capital flows or to subsidize exports in periods of economic difficulty is well-known. In the past it has been met by countervailing forces in periods of growth or by interest groups who identify themselves with a liberal international economy and who are not hurt by cyclical fluctuations. Should the current economic crisis be prolonged, the neo-nationalist forces at work are likely to create additional deterioration in the loose "truce" on both ends and means to be pursued in the international economy, and they are, therefore, worth mentioning.

POLICY COORDINATION AMONG INDUSTRIAL COUNTRIES

The emergence of neo-nationalistic tendencies in the international economic environment has heightened awareness of the need to develop better mechanisms for policy coordination. The lessons of the 1930s have never really been lost. Recognition that the Bretton Woods trade and payments system was established to avoid a recurrence of beggar-thy-neighbor policies has not prevented that system from deteriorating in the changed circumstances of the 1970s. As has often been noted, ad hoc mechanisms for policy coordination have, in fact, developed during the past decade and a half, especially within the OECD (Organization for Economic

Cooperation and Development) area whose members continue to exercise predominance in the international economy. Indeed, if the principal members of the OECD were able to coordinate their politics, it is clear that they could provide a steering mechanism for the wider international economy. (20)

However, policy coordination has been less easy than many observers would want it to be. Many factors explain the failure of policy coordination to date. First, the United States no longer has the authority or capacity to impose economic guidelines or to enforce them. A world that is becoming more multi-polar and pluralistic is simply incompatible with economic hegemony. Historical experience does not warrant optimism that a group of governments will be able to adjust their interests in compatible ways without the pressure of strong international leadership by one state.

Second, even if the OECD area proves itself to be a proper framework within which coordination could occur, the industrialized countries that comprise it have interests that overlap but do not wholly coincide. Pressures from without or within the industrialized world make it difficult for even its members to resolve their "prisoners" dilemma. European and Japanese vulnerability to pressures from OPEC or the larger but less developed south remain permanently greater than America's, and their relatively weak military capacity and lower level of economic self-sufficiency leave them with "no trumps, no luck, and no will," to borrow Stanley Hoffman's phrase. (21) Fear of the consequences of cooperating openly with the United States in today's extraordinary circumstances impedes policy cooperation. The OECD area, however tightly knit and however common the values of its members, appears to be too open to make coordination viable.

Third, the very governments that should now be assuming major responsibility for policy coordination have, for domestic purposes, been unable to generate what can loosely be termed the necessary political will. Industrialized societies have been undergoing challenges to the legitimate authority of elected governments that have made it difficult, if not impossible, for them to exercise the options at their disposal. (22) Even recent hopes that an inner core of seven (the United States, Japan, West Germany, France, Britain, Canada, and Italy) or five (the seven minus Canada and Italy) or three (the five minus France and Britain) could form the proper core for coordination have been dashed (Trilateral Commission 1976; Atlantic Council 1977). Weak governments simply cannot make the sacrifices of some domestic policy options which continue to appear to be the major costs of, and impediments to, cooperation.

Finally, policy coordination has not taken place because no one really understands what it would entail. The term seems to defy technical definition; and, even when efforts to define it succeed, it remains unclear how far the governments involved need to go, and in what areas, to make coordination successful. This impediment, which is far more intellectual than political in character, is strengthened by uncertainties over what the appropriate responses to today's problems should be. It is clear that the macro-economic and growth policies of the major participants require coordination in global economic activities. In an interdependent world, domestic governmental policies affect, and are affected by, domestic policies pursued elsewhere. (23) Stagflation has challenged the existing state of knowledge of how to control inflation and employment. Economic activities are simply not responding to what were once assumed to be valid assumptions governing macro-economic policies. (24) So long as demand management is riddled with so many uncertainties at the national level, prudence dictates that governments pursue conservative policies abroad, which translate into modest efforts at international harmonization at best.

Negative Versus Positive Cooperation

Modest efforts at harmonization or coordination are not necessarily unimportant. In fact, the history of policy coordination is one of modest but important efforts. These efforts can be understood in terms of the distinction between positive and negative cooperation. (25) As opposed to positive cooperation which involves agreement on targets to be achieved or instruments to be used, negative cooperation involves either the dismantling of obstacles to economic integration - border controls such as quotas and taxes, or internal measures such as subsidies - or agreement not to impose new obstacles.

The history of economic cooperation has essentially involved the first sort of negative cooperation - the removal of obstacles to what can loosely be called economic integration. The history of tariff dismantlement under the GATT is, perhaps, the most successful and general attempt at policy cooperation to date, although its objectives did not include international economic integration. It was designed both to improve global welfare by enhancing international trade and to remove from the arsenal of foreign policy instruments those economic border controls which, because they were used for general foreign policy purposes, fed into economic nationalism and political conflict.

A special case of this first type of negative policy cooperation is, of course, the framework of the Rome Treaty. (26) To be sure, the European Communities embody a number of important steps toward positive co-operation, most notably in the Common Agriculture Policy. However, the European Communities have always been a special instance of negative cooperation, aiming to create a customs union embodying a free trade area. The European Communities are special in that an explicit aim has been economic integration and not simply the elimination of barriers to trade.

A second type of negative policy cooperation pertains to commitments not to raise barriers to international flows of goods and services or to the mobile factors of production, especially technology and capital. Pledges taken by OECD countries to avoid use of tariffs as a means of dealing with balance-of-payment problems arising out of the increased deficits due to oil price rises is an important form of negative cooperation of this sort. The refusal to impose such barriers is especially significant as a form of policy cooperation right now when governments, confronting deficits, inflation, and unemployment at home, would want to use border controls as a means of dealing with their problems, and when so much uncertainty surrounds the effectiveness and applicability of Keynesian demand management practices considered valid a decade ago.

Neither form of negative cooperation is adequate to assure policy cooperation in the middle or long run. Unless buttressed by positive forms of cooperation, negative forms carry with them the seeds of their own destruction. At best, they represent short-term solutions for the achievement of governmental objectives. The removal of barriers, for example, leads almost automatically to economic integration whether or not that is the aim of governments in eliminating or reducing them. Once barriers to trade are eliminated, hidden barriers become important as their effects on trade, either by impeding it or by appearing unfair, become almost automatically politicized. Yet, there is no reason to assume that the problems they thus pose will necessarily lead to the forms of engrenage once envisioned by functionalist thinkers. The economic truce that characterized pledges not to impose new barriers is, at best, short-term. Unless solutions are found to relieve those pressures that give rise to the neo-mercantilist tendencies that underlay the economic truce, the truce will likely give way to them.

The Domestic Role of Policy Cooperation

Policy cooperation is too often regarded as a technical means to facilitate the handling of essentially international problems, yet policy cooperation is not likely to work unless it serves the domestic ends of the governments involved. That is to say, cooperation, and especially positive cooperation, will be feasible for governments if, and only if, through it governments perceive that they will be better able to deal with domestic problems or to bolster support from certain interest groups and minimize opposition from others.

The importance of the domestic aspects of policy cooperation should not be underestimated. This is especially the case today when all governments seem to be undergoing crises, or at least fundamental challenges to their own authority. (27) As governments seek new ways to bolster their authority, they will seek out new modes of policy cooperation if through it their capacity to carry out their domestic objectives is enhanced.

Generalizations concerning the domestic political benefits of international economic policy cooperation ought not, however, to be made in too facile a way. Non-cooperation can also bring benefits to governmental authority under certain circumstances. The mixed-motive aspects of cooperation/ non-cooperation can be seen in an examination of some of the political characteristics of recent summit meetings among major industrialized countries over issues of policy cooperation. At the first such summit in France in the fall of 1975, the motivations of both the German and French governments for requesting the summit were mixed. Both governments, but especially the German, wanted to use the meeting to bolster their sagging domestic support by demonstrating that their economic problems could be handled only by joint action with the United States. Both governments also were in a no-lose situation in that they could blame the American government for what they might have considered to be inappropriate policies or lack of willingness to cooperate. In such circumstances, they won regardless of the outcome of the summit. Had the United States government agreed to adopt expansionary policies to help them induce export-led growth, they could have pointed to their success in pressuring the United States. If the United States government failed to adopt policies that they considered desirable, they could have blamed the failure of their economic recovery programs on President Ford. Much of the same political ambience surrounded the most recent summit in London at the the beginning of the Carter administration.

The politics of summitry ought not, however, lead us to miss the major point of this section which is quite simple. Policy cooperation will not work unless it entails substantial political benefits to governments in their national political arenas. These benefits can be short-term, as has been the case in recent summits, or they can be longer-term, as has been the case with the long-standing reliance of successive American administrations upon GATT commitments as a means of warding off protectionist interest groups and their influence in the Congress.

Scope of Policy Coordination

One major set of questions about policy coordination relates to how much coordination is required, under what circumstances, and involving what sorts of policy instruments. Although a number of typologies of policy coordination have been suggested, I find a recent analysis put forward by Haas and Ruggie to be especially suggestive. (28) Although they are concerned more with the construction of international regimes than with the analysis of economic policy coordination, what they say seems applicable to any system of interdependent relationships. Haas and Ruggie define the following major functions that regimes perform, each of which can also be viewed as a type of policy coordination:

1. Problem search and definition
2. The harmonization or standardization of national responses
3. The delimitation of property rights
4. The collective elaboration of welfare choices (i.e., the calculation of allocational trade-offs). (29)

These functions, or types of policy coordination, ascend from one to four, from the simplest form of interdependent relationship to the most complex.

A modest amount of interdependence and interrelatedness requires that governments cooperate on a minimal basis through the pooling of information and, perhaps, common evaluation of problems. This sort of policy cooperation has been undertaken since the early 1960s by the OECD Secretariat and, especially, within the OECD's Economic Policy Committee structure. Several types of activities involving policy cooperation can be subsumed under this heading. These include the pooling of data on recent economic activities to the more important sharing of information concerning short-term policy plans.

When governments commit themselves to tell their principal economic partners what they plan to do over the coming quarter or half-year, three important functions are served. First, each government is provided with an opportunity to evaluate the effects of its partners' policies on its own domestic economy and can adjust its own policies in light of this additional information.   Second, each government has the opportunity to make its partners aware of problems that it might encounter as a result of the policies they are pursuing and, perhaps, if only to a small degree, each might then convince the partners to change policies.   Finally, and perhaps most importantly, the very act of submitting one's domestic policies to the scrutiny of other governments impels a government to rationalize and make much more coherent its own short-term economic targets. It forces, in short, economic coordination at home, which is a prerequisite to economic coordination abroad.

Higher levels of interdependence require much more in the way of policy coordination - what Haas and Ruggie call harmonization or standardization. Whether the OECD countries have reached a level of economic integration which requires very much in the way of harmonization or standardization is an open question. Clearly, the members of the European Communities have reached this stage, as efforts to control the effects of a customs union have justified the harmonization of tax systems in the form of the VAT (Value-Added Tax) and standardization of licensing arrangements not simply for products but for service professions as well (e.g., physicians).

A much higher level of interdependence - one clearly not yet reached in the industrialized world today - requires what Haas and Ruggie call the delimitation of common property rights.   This requires mechanisms to define how public goods should be created and how scarce public goods should be allocated. The creation of a common currency and the delineation of how its supply should be expanded, who should have access to it, and the uses to which it should be put represent a very high degree of policy coordination indeed. In fact, from some perspectives, the creation of a common currency involves transcending the problem of coordination through the development of truly supra-national mechanisms. It is doubtful that any area of international life today is so interdependent as to require such a policy response or even to make it feasible.

Finally, an ultimate level of interdependence involves joint elaboration of welfare choices, or trade-offs, affecting the members of the community in question.   In a highly interdependent system issues tend to become increasingly linked to one another, just as a range of trade, monetary, macro-economic, and defense policy questions have become linked in the Atlantic area. As Haas and Ruggie put it, "Once functional linkages among regimes are established, issues must be considered in terms of the broader policy bundles that define the parameters and perimeters of collective concern." (30) That is to say, complexly linked issues require at least one form of centralization, the confrontation of issues and governments collectively. They need not, however, require centralized implementation of decisions. The Paris Conference on International Economic Cooperation provides an example, although the issues at stake are not as complexly linked as they would be in a highly interdependent system. The Conference has basically served as a mechanism in which collective choices could be negotiated and bargains struck across linked areas.   However, the implementation of decisions - on trade, finance and energy, for example - can take place through a variety of simpler more decentralized procedures   and mechanisms.

Policy Goals and Policy Instruments

A further useful distinction to make about policy coordination and, especially, about harmonization concerns policy goals and instruments. Without entering the impossible conundrum of when goals become means and vice-versa, it clearly makes a difference for governments whether they jointly target their objectives or what means they use to achieve them. What is not clear on a theoretical level is when it makes sense to focus on the one as opposed to the other.

It is sometimes easier for governments to coordinate policies by focusing on certain broad objectives such as reducing inflation below double digit levels or aiming at a specified lower rate of unemployment. Fixing upon common targets allows governments to invoke those instruments - fiscal, monetary, or border controls - which each finds most suitable to its special circumstances. This seems to be the way a loose form of policy coordination has been working to some degree in the Atlantic area. However, there are often cases in which major disputes, sometimes of an ideological nature, emerge from any effort to target objectives. In recent years it has become somewhat impossible to achieve agreement across the Atlantic on such issues as the causes of inflation or the principles of a proper international monetary system.   When such theological disputes impede   the achievement of consensus on goals, focusing on instruments is often the only way to achieve a modicum of cooperation.   Out of pragmatism, consensus on appropriate instruments can serve as proximate or proxy goals, as governments jointly try to reach common ground. Indeed, reform of the monetary system seems to be proceeding along these lines. If, a decade from now, the major monetary powers begin jointly to target their exchange rates and to support those rates, it will matter little to an observing Martian whether one group calls the system a "managed float" and another calls it "a return to fixed rates."

Miscellaneous Distinctions

Any systematic examination of what constitutes policy coordination should involve the elaboration of a typology of different types of policies based on the functions they serve (employment or price levels, for example) or the instruments they involve (e.g., monetary or fiscal) or their designated area - transportation or regional development.   While such an analysis is beyond the scope of this essay, three further general observations seem in order at the present time.

The first concerns linkages. It has often been observed that the linkage of so many countries to so many others, and so many policy instruments to so many others, has led to a sort of paralysis in today's international economy. Policy actions, domestically or internationally, can readily be neutralized by their own effects or by the actions of others. Yet linkage can also serve as a basis for international agreement. This is especially the case when different governments seek different goals, which often makes it easier for them to trade-off their preferences through international cooperation. In working out agreements, Germany's preference for lower inflation and higher unemployment might well be traded against the French preference for lower unemployment and higher inflation.

The second observation concerns the general state of the international conjoncture. Again, an important but banal point is involved: Policy coordination is likely to be most successful in periods when economic diversity is notable and when economic cycles are out of phase. It is also more successful, or at least more feasible, in periods of sustained economic growth such as the one characterized by the 1960s. Coordination is extremely difficult when the economies are in phase and in recession simultaneously since none is then in a position to induce growth elsewhere by increasing its imports from the others.

The final observation concerns the current state of what might be called the Kantian problem: whether republics can join together to create a system of perpetual peace. Kant's argument had to do with the pacific nature of republics as well as with the belief that a natural harmony of interests exists among them, which is enhanced by increases in international commerce. Trade creates a stake for all governments in increasing internationalism. This belief is predicated on the notion that commerce benefits everyone by increasing the wealth of all trading partners, thus reinforcing the pacific nature of republic governments.

The governments of the industrialized non-Communist world loosely fit Kant's description. I need not at this point enumerate the long list of common features that describe them, from social structures and social goals to shared cultural traditions; but, most important among these, perhaps, has been the development of similar structures for economic management. This has had a dual set of effects which impinges on both the desirability and feasibility of international harmonization of economic policies. First, as I alluded to earlier, the various national economies are administered according to what Geiger has called the "neo-national rule of experts," who see their own personal advance intertwined with the economic growth of their own societies. (31) This interweaving of personal and general welfare places an emphasis on the desirability of national autonomy in decision-making. "National economic policies," as Cooper has argued, "rely for their effectiveness on the separation of markets. This is true of monetary policy, of income taxation, of regulatory policies, and of redistributive policies (whether the last to be through differential taxation or through direct transfers)." (32) Governments, in short, have a penchant to opt for second-best solutions in which national autonomy need not be sacrificed. Second, the convergence of domestic economic structures has meant that the governments of the Industrialized West are now pursuing similar goals. And this pursuit, paradoxically, may well create difficulties for international cooperation if we assume that cooperation is based largely on the ability of different governments to strike satisfactory bargains with one another. Successful bargaining normally requires that governments trade off different sorts of goals.

CONCLUSIONS

The politics of policy cooperation clearly involves the need to tame lurking economic nationalism. It is also filled with many political unknowns, some of which were outlined in the earlier sections of this essay. We are living in a world in which great pressures exist from the major economic powers of the West to institutionalize consultations on demand management policies, especially if progress is not made on major substantive issues. Here, institutionalization will become symbolically meaningful, if substantively empty. A principal aim of some governments today is to create a forum in which they can have a voice in influencing the course of American domestic economic policies.

For some years the European governments, especially the French, have hesitated to join with the United States in any regularized series of meetings, since they have viewed the establishment of a common institution with the United States as a mechanism whereby the United States could impede the processes of European economic integration. It now seems that many governments have changed their minds. They have discovered that European economic integration cannot be fostered without also taking into account the direction of domestic and foreign economic policy in the United States. They can foster harmonization within Europe more efficiently by taking into account the nature of American economic policy than by placing themselves in opposition to the United States. The United States government - and others as well - ought to hesitate before they regularize such an arrangement.

While it now seems to be the case that consultations among the governments of the United States, Japan, Britain, France, and West Germany can more efficiently resolve differences over the management of common problems than can any other grouping of governments, it is not necessarily the case that the same grouping will be the right one for problems that might arise three, five, or ten years from now. Since we are in a situation of great flux in which other governments might supersede this particular grouping, governments should wait until a more appropriate time to make a decision concerning which of them are to be the principals involved in policy coordination in a formally institutionalized way.

Consultations will, however, proceed, just as they have up to now. They should focus on two major types of problems: short-range stabilization policies, where consultation among five governments is appropriate; and longer-range issues involved in the steering of the global economy, where coordination among industrialized societies will have a significant and critical effect. However, until many of the political and intellectual unknowns are resolved, no permanent institutional mechanisms should be developed.

NOTES

(1) Pierre Hassner, "The New Europe: From Cold War to Hot Peace," International Journal, 27 (Winter 1971-72), p. 31.

(2) Ernst B. Haas, Beyond the Nation-State: Functionalism and International Organization (Stanford, Calif: Stanford University Press, 1964); Edward L. Morse, "The Politics of Interdependence," International Organization, 23:2 (Spring 1969), pp. 311-326; Edward L. Morse, "The Transformation of Foreign Policies: Modernization, Externalization and Interdependence," World Politics 22:3 (April 1970), pp. 371-392; and Edward L. Morse Foreign Policy and Interdependence in Gaullist France (Princeton, New Jersey: Princeton University Press, 1973).

(3) Edward L. Morse, Modernization and the Transformation of International Relations (New York: Free Press, 1976); and Simon Kuznets, Modern Economic Growth: Rate, Structure and Spread (New Haven, Conn.: Yale University Press, 1966).

(4) Klaus Knorr, On the Uses of Military Power in the Nuclear Age (Princeton, N,J.: Princeton University Press, 1966).

(5) Jacques Pelkmans, The Process of Economic Integration (Tilburg: Tilburg University, 1975).

(6) Richard N. Cooper, The Economics of Interdependence (New York: McGraw Hill/Council on Foreign Relations, 1968); Richard N. Cooper, "Economic Interdependence and Foreign Policy in the Seventies," World Politics, 24:2 (January 1972); Richard N. Cooper, "Trade Policy is Foreign Policy," Foreign Policy (Winter 1971-72); Robert Keohane and Joseph Nye, "World Politics and the International Economic System," in The Future of the International Economic Order: An Agenda for Research, ed. C. Fred Bergsten (Lexington, Mass.: Lexington Heath, 1973); Keohane and Nye, Power and Interdependence (Boston: Little Brown, 1977); Ernst B. Haas and John Ruggie, "Beyond Incrementalism and Holism," Berkeley, California (mimeo), 1975.

(7) Morse, Modernization and the Transformation of International Relations op. cit.

(8) Charles P. Kindleberger, The World in Depression, 1929-1939 (Berkeley, California: University of California Press, 1973).

(9) Jacques Pelkmans, op. cit., pp. 50-51.

(10) Theodore Geiger, The Fortunes of the West (Bloomington, Indiana: Indiana University Press, 1973).

(11) John Hicks, The Theory of Economic History (London: Oxford University Press, 1969), p. 162.

(12) Pelkmans, op. cit., p. 51.

(13) Edward L. Morse, "Political Choice and Alternative Monetary Regimes," in Alternatives to Monetary Disorder, by Fred Hirsch and Michael Doyle, and Edward L. Morse (New York: McGraw-Hill/Council on Foreign Relations, 1977).

(14) Geiger, op. cit., p. 3.

(15) Harry Johnson, "General Principles for World Monetary Reform," in In Search of a New World Economic Order, ed. Hugh Corbet and Robert Jackson (London: Croom Helm, 1974), p. 162.

(16) Joan Robinson, The New Mercantilism (London: Cambridge University Press, 1966), p. 3.

(17) Cooper, "Economic Interdependence and Foreign Policy in the Seventies," op. cit.

(18) Hans O. Schmitt, "The International Monetary System: Three Options for Reform," in International Affairs (London) 50:2 (April 1974).

(19) Ernest H. Preeg, Economic Blocs and U.S. Foreign Policy (Washington, D.C.: National Planning Association, 1974), p. 152.

(20) Miriam C. Camps, The Management of Interdependence: A Preliminary View (New York: Council on Foreign Relations, 1974).

(21) Stanley Hoffmann, "No Trumps, No Luck, No Will: Gloomy Thoughts on Europe's Plight," in Atlantis Lost: U.S-European Relations After the Cold War (New York: New York University Press, 1976), pp. 1-46.

(22) Morse, Modernization and the Transformation of International Relations, op. cit.

(23) Cooper, The Economics of Interdependence, op. cit.

(24) Ralph Bryant, Interdependence and the Theory of Economic Policy Washington, D.C.: The Brookings Institution (mimeo), 1977.

(25) Jacques Pelkmans, "Economic Cooperation Among Western Countries" (New York: Council on Foreign Relations (mimeo) 1977).

(26) John Pinder, "Positive and Negative Integration: Some Problems of Economic Union in the EEC," in The World Today (March 1968).

(27) Pierre Hassner, "The New Europe: From Cold War to Hot Peace," International Journal, 27 (Winter 1971-72).

(28) Haas and Ruggie, op. cit.

(29) Ibid, pp. 4-6.

(30) Ibid, p. 11.

(31) Geiger, op. cit.

(32) Cooper, op. cit.

The New Nationalism and
Sub-National Regionalism

7 Quebec Foreign Policy? Canada and Ethno-Regionalism
Robert J. Jackson
Abina M. Dann

INTRODUCTION

The manifestations of ethnic-nationalism and sub-national regionalism in the issue-area of foreign policy, and their possible effects at the international level, are rarely discussed systematically in political science. This is understandable given that little data has been collected which lends itself easily to such analysis. However, recent developments in certain sub-national regionalist movements in Britain, Belgium, Canada, and elsewhere suggest that it is time to initiate a debate on foreign policy and ethno-regionalism. Besides facilitating a more comprehensive understanding of this general phenomenon, such a perspective will allow an examination of the impact of the New Nationalism in the North Atlantic area.

This paper touches on three broad subjects. First, analytical approaches drawn from comparative and international politics are put forward. Second, a discussion follows on the evolving international competence of the province of Quebec. This section is intended to illustrate the potential impact which an ethno-regional movement may have on the internal and external coordinating capabilities of central government. The third, and concluding section, emphasizes at a general level the importance of analyzing ethno-regional trends in the area of foreign policy, and suggests some of the implications of sub-national trends within the interdependent context of the North Atlantic area.

* We would like to thank Kim Nossal, Professor of Political Science at McMaster University, and Peyton V. Lyon, Professor of Political Science at Carleton University, for commenting on an earlier draft of this paper.

APPROACHES TO ANALYZING ETHNO-REGIONAL FOREIGN POLICIES

Two traditions in political science are related to the question posed in this paper. In the study of ethno-regional groups and foreign policy, comparative politics and international politics approaches touch and even overlap.

A Comparative Politics Perspective

Comparative politics specialists analyze ethno-regionalism with varying objectives. Traditionally there has been an effort to identify those components of ethnicity which may give rise to nationalist aspirations, for instance, common language, history, culture, religion, and territory. (1) The additional aim of such writers as Enloe and Mayo, and the primary goal of another group of authors, has been to identify the interplay of such factors and to use them to explain the configuration of domestic politics. (2) Recently there has been a new interest in examining the possible reasons for the resurgence of nationalism in the developed industrialized world. (3) This collection of authors elaborates on the role which such factors as modernization, economic development, integration, assimilation, class, and party may play in fermenting nationalist fervor among sub-national units. As with the first group of analysts, ethno-nationalism is employed as a dependent variable.

Finally, throughout the literature on ethnicity and nationalism definitions have been offered which attempt to make precise distinctions between the various terms. For example, the terms "ethnic" and "people" generally refer to social groups which consciously share some aspects of common culture and are defined primarily by descent. (4) The word "nation" is used to denote any self-conscious people, whereas the term "state" identifies the formal political organization which grants citizenship to its members. The term "nation-state" should identify the coterminous existence of one people within the boundaries of a territorial state. Such an exact usage of the expression has unfortunately proved the exception rather than the rule. (5)

The approaches and definitions described above may assist in the development of ideas about ethno-regional foreign policy. The definitional clarifications in particular may be used to determine which ethnic nationalisms remain in the people category of complementary existence within a state, and which movements are identifiable as aspiring to the nation-state alternative. If it were possible to make such precise conceptual distinctions among these terms, then in the future it might prove possible to associate types of foreign policies with different kinds of ethno-regional movements. This paper is more modest in its intentions, but it does initiate a discussion along this comparative politics/international relations orientation.

An International Relations Perspective

International relations theory has not traditionally been concerned with the effect of sub-national politics within an international context. The state unit is treated as the primary source of foreign policy output into the international system. This approach does not recognize the potential effect which ethno-regional foreign policy may have at both the state and supra-state levels of analysis.

A recent theoretical trend, initiated by James N. Rosenau, has attempted, however, to develop concepts which will permit integrated cross-systems analysis of sub-national, state, and supra-national phenomena. In his work the author develops the concept of linkage, which is defined as "any recurrent sequence of behavior that originates in one system and is reacted to in another." (6) The linkage itself is seen as a basic unit of analysis consisting of direct or indirect inputs and outputs between the state and the international environment. Some outputs, conventionally called foreign policy, are designed to bring about responses in other systems. (7)

There is nothing in the concept of linkage to prevent it from being extended to include consideration of sub-national outputs. For instance, in some cases initiatives by ethno-regional groups might be classified as nascent foreign policy behavior. Certain sub-national outputs could have an effect at the state and international levels. These sub-national units could, in turn, be subject to inputs from other sources. Thus, it might be possible to identify certain patterns of interaction among these three levels and make some generalizations concerning behavior. To date, however, little substantive empirical work has been accomplished in this field and virtually none has been related to the phenomenon of ethno-regionalism. Considerable time and data will be needed in order to establish the form and intensity of those behavioral sequences which would indicate whether significant linkages actually do exist among international, state, and sub-national levels.

Tentative Suggestions for Analyzing Ethno-regional Foreign Policies

In order to classify sub-nationalist groups according to their foreign policies, it is necessary to select a definition which does not assume that all international actors are independent states. For this reason foreign policy here will be considered as those discrete actions employed by communities with the intention of changing the behavior of other states and adjusting their own activities to the international environment. (8) In discussing a community's foreign policy, it may be useful to distinguish between foreign policy articulation and posturing, and that type of activity which engenders not only domestic but also international consequences. Foreign polcy, then, is indicated by statements of position in official documents or publications associated with a sub-national group, by intended or actual commitment in the areas of defense and bilateral state relations, and by participation in bilateral and multilateral commissions or bureaus. In the case of Quebec it has become evident that its policy has moved increasingly from the realm of posturing to that of activity as the strength of the nationalist movement has grown over the past 15 years.

One might classify ethno-regional foreign policy according to a progressive differentiation in the group's perception of its possibility of becoming a nation-state in its own right. Three major categories are suggested by such a factor.

In the first and most primitive category might be found all the groups, movements, and so on which exist within any polity but which have no particular concern to be called a nation or a state. Such groups, however, may be recognized as having ethnic interests which do extend beyond the borders of the state. While such ethnic clusters may not have any territorial claims within the domestic context, they might attempt to exercise foreign influence through the state apparatus. This category would include such groups as the Ukrainians in Canada, the American Irish, or the Romanis in several European countries, all of whose actions influence national foreign policy within a broad context.

The second category includes those ethnic groups or peoples who maintain a territorial identification within the state. Demands for regional autonomy are usually associated with a certain degree of self-governance within the boundaries of this territory. The limiting principle of this category is that its members make their demands within the final context of belonging to the existing state. A multitude of examples could be used to illustrate this category: the Québécois nationalist movement from 1961-75, the Inuit and Dene (Canada), the moderate Basques and Catalans (Spain), the Bretons, Basques, Alsacians, and Corsicans (France), the Flemish and Wallons (Belgium), and the Slovenes (Austria). Such groups may exercise an indirect foreign policy output because of their strong impact on the central foreign policy process. It is hypothesized that because ethno-regional groups in this category respect the limiting principle of the state, their demands are more likely to be placed within the practical restraints imposed by the state's foreign policy. It is unlikely, for example, that the Jura movement would develop a foreign policy which was incompatible with established Swiss neutrality.

The third and last category includes the independentist ethno-regional movements. Of course, part of an historical movement may fall into category two while another part falls into category three, such as has occurred in Quebec history and in the present day Basque national movement. Because they are statist-oriented, category three movements are not bound by the limiting principle of belonging to the state. Their actions are circumscribed, however, by the practical considerations of the boundaries inherent in larger regional and international communities. Sub-national regionalist groups (which tend to be well organized) in this category would include the Parti Québécois (PQ), the Basque Euzkadi Ta Azatasuna (ETA), the Scottish Nationalist Party (SNP), the Plaid Cymru Welsh, and the Croatians in Yugoslavia. Groups in this category have direct foreign policy outputs in the form of intended commitments and possibly in the area of foreign policy activity. Statist-oriented foreign policy initiatives by such ethno-regional movements are likely to be considered unacceptable to existing states. Thus, while in theory movement in this category may make more comprehensive demands since they are not bound by the state's foreign policy, these requests are more likely to meet with opposition because of the fundamental threat they pose to the existing political framework. How effective ethno-regional foreign policies would be if independence were achieved is a matter for speculation. The parameters affecting behavior, however, could be expected to differ substantially from those existing in the previous state. Although not necessary for our purposes, a further category four could be added which would be comprised of any political entities which become recognized internationally as independent states.

Other well publicized groups in the Atlantic area, which might be classified in the above categories include the Cornish and Manx (the United Kingdom), the Friulians (Yugoslavia), the Savoyards (France), the Armenians (Turkey), the Frisians (the Netherlands), the Laplanders (Finland), the people of the Faeroe Islands (Denmark), and certain linguistic groups found in Norway.

Another approach to classifying ethno-regional foreign policies would be to examine their actions along a dimension running in scope from limited articulation to extensive activity. The characteristic which would identify an ethnic group as articulating a foreign policy would be the extent to which such an entity desired to become an international actor. Such an orientation would permit one to examine the aspirations of sub-national groups. However, judgments about psychological dispositions are beyond the range of this paper. Moreover, an appropriate classification system with exhaustive and mutually exclusive categories cannot be constructed at this introductory stage in the development of comparative politics and international relations perspectives on ethno-regionalism and foreign policy.

The strength of many category three sub-national movements appears to have increased in the past decade. This is certainly true of Quebec whose case will now be discussed in detail in order to bring out some distinctions between the second and third categories of the classification. An acquaintance with those manifestations of Quebec ethno-regionalism related to the area of foreign policy may illustrate the effect which any ethno-regional movement could have on the internal and external capabilities of a state.

QUEBEC AND FOREIGN POLICY

Where Does the Nation Meet the State?

The province of Quebec fell into the second category of our classification during the years 1960-1975. During that time increasing demands for cultural and linguistic sovereignty were made by the province. The general thrust was for special status within the Confederation of Canada. The federal government attempted to accommodate the French faction with constitutional reviews, "cooperative federalism," nation-wide support for a program of bilingualism and biculturalism, and increased recruitment of francophones to higher positions in the central government. However, Ottawa was unwilling to allow Quebec special status, largely because it would make relations more difficult with the nine other provinces. The apparent inability of the federal government to adjust to mounting nationalist demands, and what Prime Minister Trudeau refers to as the "obtuseness" of English-Canada in accommodating two languages, did nothing to discourage the growing appeal of an active nationalist movement in Quebec. (9)

The growth of separatism in Quebec is undisputed. If a graph of the votes for separatist parties were drawn it would indicate a definite trend in the direction of independence. In 1966 the first separatist parties, Le Ralliement National and Le Ralliement pour l'Indépendance Nationale, gained only 10% of the popular vote. Compared to these earlier parties, the younger Parti Québécois demonstrated remarkable growth potential, in the 1970 election it obtained 24% of the popular vote. In 1973 this figure increased to 30%, and in 1976 it was 41%.

At its inception in 1968 the independentist Parti Québécois brought to the nationalist movement an explicitly statist orientation. (10) Since this party acceded to power in the provincial election of November 15, 1976, the ethno-regional movement in Quebec has increasingly begun to fall into the third category, that of a nation seeking independent state status within the international community. In the development of an independentist platform PQ party documents have included explicit reference to foreign policy objectives in the areas of economic union, defense, and participation in the international community.

While the PQ has provided a more extensive articulation of foreign policy goals than the autonomist-oriented nationalist movement, foreign policy output, and its indirect impact, is no stranger to the Quebec scene. Since the early 1960s Quebec has demonstrated an international competence in certain fields, particularly in the development of relations with francophonie comprised of France, Belgium, and the French-speaking states of Africa and the West Indies. The Department of Federal-Provincial Affairs established in 1961, renamed the Department of Intergovernmental Affairs in 1967, is responsible for the exercise of Quebec's international dimension.

With this department acting as liaison, Quebec has come to participate in numerous trans-national agreements. In 1964, an agreement was concluded by the Youth Minister of Quebec and ASTEP (Association pour l'organisation des stages en France). This arrangement developed a progressively economic emphasis and, as a reflection of this, in 1969 it was renamed ACTIM-MAIQ (Association de coopération technique, économique, et industrielle - Ministère des Affaires Inter-gouvernementales du Quebec). This accord has continued to be active in encouraging economic and industrial cooperation between France and Quebec in the areas of energy and resource development. (11) Quebec also takes part in the activities of such institutions as the International Association of French-Speaking Parliamentarians and the Association des universités partiellement ou entièrement de langue francaise (AUPELF). There is extensive Quebec cooperation in promoting professional, student, and project-personnel exchanges with the French-speaking world through such agencies as the Office franco-québécois de la jeunesse, CIDA, and CUSO. (12) In 1970 Quebec set an intriguing precedent by becoming a "participating government" in the francophone Agence de coopération culturelle et technique (ACCT). Jean-Marc Leger, a Québécois, became this organization's first Secretary-General. At the bilateral level, since the opening in 1961 of a General Delegation in Paris Quebec has distributed delegations and trade missions in other countries. Provincial representatives are stationed in London, Brussels, Milan, Rome, Dusseldorf, New York, Boston, Chicago, Dallas, Los Angeles, Lafayette, Tokyo, Beirut, Abidjan, and Port-au-Prince. (13) Since the visits to France of Premier Jean Lesage in 1961 and 1974, there have been frequent exchanges of highly placed French and Quebec government officials in order to discuss matters of mutual concern.

By far the most memorable trip of a French official to Canada was that of President Charles de Gaulle in July, 1967. While addressing a crowd in front of Montreal City Hall the President was reportedly overwhelmed by the same sentiments he experienced during the liberation of France in 1944. This moved him to cry, "Vive le Quebec libre!" The following day, July 25th, Prime Minister Lester B. Pearson publicly reprimanded de Gaulle, describing his statement as "unacceptable to the Canadian government and its people." The French leader cancelled his protocol visit to Ottawa, returning abruptly to Paris. Later the same year in Quebec City a joint communique was issued by Premier Daniel Johnson and then French Education Minister Alain Peyrefitte. It outlined new educational and cultural exchange programs which had been worked out between the signatories.

At first, Quebec's increasingly autonomous intergovernmental initiative did not affect Canadian external affairs capability. Once initial difficulties had been overcome through the establishment of ad hoc arrangements, it was hoped that the provincial liaisons might constitute a complementary extension of Canadian foreign policy. However, the federal government never sanctioned the notion that in partaking in this form of international behavior Quebec was also imbued with jurisdictional competence, although some Quebec officials attempted to foster the attitude that the provincial state was establishing through precedents a permanent status.

Significant differences developed in federal and provincial conceptions of the appropriate exercise of Quebec's international dimension. In May 1967 Canada signed a cultural accord with Belgium. For several years the provincial government had entertained the idea of establishing a similar agreement, and had already held official talks to discuss the subject. Informed at the eleventh hour that Ottawa was going to sign an accord (which would make no special provision for provincial participation as an earlier 1965 Franco-Canadian blanket agreement had intended to do), the Premier of Quebec expressed astonishment that a solemn agreement considered to affect areas of provincial jurisdiction should be planned without previous consultation with Quebec. For this reason the provincial government chose to dissociate itself from the federal action, with the result that the signed accord has developed little content due to lack of Quebec participation. (15)

Another collision over acceptable international participation by Quebec occurred at an international French-speaking conference on education at Libreville, Gabon in 1968. Quebec was invited to attend the gathering on an equal basis with other participants, although the latter were sovereign states. In response to this unexpected transaction, executed largely with French intervention, the Canadian government instructed its Ambassador-Designate to Gabon not to present his credentials. Following this incident, Ottawa persuaded the countries involved to agree to a "new normalization" of Quebec relations with francophone states and institutions so that unorthodox procedures would not be repeated. (16)

As provincial activities with an international expression became more numerous, and as the strength and articulation of the independentist movement grew stronger, Ottawa found it necessary to define in writing the limits to Quebec's international initiatives. The 1968 White Papers entitled "Federalism and International Relations" and "Federalism and International Conferences on Education" were evidence of this. As the first of these papers pointed out, Canada has been placed in an unusual position compared with other federal states. The federal authorities have the power to enter into treaties, but the Parliament of Canada is unable to enact legislation implementing such agreements when the subject matter falls within provincial jurisdiction. (17) In these documents, however, the federal government stated categorically that Canada's external sovereignty is indivisible. This position has been recognized internationally - emphatically by the United States, more reservedly by France.

At the domestic level, too, the demands of the maturing nationalist movement have tended to make the business of governance even more complex. For instance, in the absence of federal acceptance of a newly defined "special status" for Quebec, that province has consistently vetoed motions at federal-provincial conferences which call for the repatriation of the Canadian constitution and other efforts at comprehensive constitutional change. In this way Quebec has contributed effectively to keeping federal-provincial cooperation in a fundamental stalemate. The problems of renegotiating the Canadian Confederation are not easily solved, as Stairs notes. "It is difficult in any case to know how far the process of decentralization could proceed without triggering an irreversible drift towards a final fragmentation and disintegration of the political, economic, social, and psychological foundations of the Canadian 'union' as they are felt at home and perceived abroad." (18)

The Parti Québécois and Foreign Policy

With the accession to power of the independentist PQ government in November 1976 the Canadian government's acceptance of Quebec's international role has become more sensitive and cautious. In a very short period Ottawa and the provincial government have clashed several times, reflecting increased tension over the issues of the indivisibility of Canada's external sovereignty and Quebec's foreign policy presence. An element of strain in Ottawa-Quebec perspectives on foreign relations was apparent during the consecutive visits to France of Quebec Minister of Intergovernmental Affairs, Claude Morin, and Prime Minister Trudeau. In April 1977 the PQ government's Morin was given a warm welcome by some French officials, particularly the Mayor of Paris, Jacques Chirac, who assured the Quebec government of Gaullist support for its independence aims. In May Trudeau was given a more restrained, though proper, reception.

In the summer of 1977 further incidents demonstrated the stress in the federal-provincial area of foreign policy activity. On July 15, 1977 Le Devoir reported that the 10th Assembly of the Association internationale des parlementaires de langue francaise (AIPLF) held in Paris was a "catastrophe" for Canada. Gérard Laniel, Vice-President of the federal House of Commons, stated that he and his delegation were greatly dissatisfied with their reception by the French government. The privileged treatment accorded the Quebec delegation, led by Clément Richard, President of the Quebec National

Assembly, was particularly evident in a speech given by President Valéry Giscard d'Estaing that surprised the Canadian delegation. The unamused Mr. Laniel announced that his delegation had no intention, however, of retiring from the Association.

The French Consul-General Henri Dumont attended a ceremony in Montreal on July 24 commemorating de Gaulle's 1967 Vive le Quebec libre! speech. External Affairs Minister Don Jamieson indicated that he would have preferred to have had the French official stay away. An official in the PMO's office later stated, "It is not a bad thing to commemorate the failings of an otherwise great man (de Gaulle) and as for the consul-general, our ambassador in Paris keeps attending commemorative ceremonies of the liberation of France." (19)

On July 25, 1977 Quebec Minister of Intergovernmental Affairs Claude Morin accused federal Minister of Industry and Commerce Jean Chrétien of being a "political hack." In asking a provincial government representative to delay a planned visit to Iran until the Federal Minister's visit was completed, Morin considered that Chretien was trying to take credit for a direct Quebec-Iran contract totalling $37 million. (20)

On July 27, 1977 the PQ government released documents showing continuing disagreement and tension with Ottawa over Quebec's dealings with the European Economic Community. Quebec had requested a role in the Sub-Committee on Industrial Development which decides possible fields of industrial cooperation between Canada and the Community. The Sub-committee was to meet in May 1977. Despite repeated requests during the winter, Quebec was not informed of the details of the meeting in time to participate. Ottawa offered to have an official participant meet with representatives from Ontario and Quebec after the meeting, but Quebec rejected this arrangement. Consequently, the province refused to sit on other sub-committees until an acceptable federal decision regarding Quebec's participation in all sub-committees would be made. (21)

In a September 1977 visit to Canada the actions of French Minister of Justice Alain Peyrefitte were viewed with some reservation in the federal capital. While in Quebec to celebrate the tenth anniversary of the first Quebec-France cultural agreement, Peyrefitte signed a reciprocal judicial agreement with Quebec Minister of Justice Marc-André Bédard. The French Minister's conduct was unsettling to many committed federalists disturbed by the state of Canadian unity.

The PQ nationalist party has also encouraged more informal international communications with other ethno-regional movements. For instance, Le Jour, a twice monthly tabloid associated with the PQ has featured articles on the Jura, Breton, and Scottish nationalist movements. In response to a growing interest in Quebec abroad, arrangements were made by the Quebec government in July 1977 to implement a program of Quebec studies at the University of Trier in Germany.

Subsequent developments have not held much promise that dissension between Ottawa and Quebec over the latter's international role will fade. On October 25, 1977 the federal government announced that it was seriously thinking about assuming the leadership of a francophone commonwealth which would embrace those partly or totally French-speaking states. Jean-Pierre Goyer, Minister of Supply and Services, who was newly responsible for

Canadian relations with francophone countries, revealed that the proposed commonwealth would be patterned after the existing British model. Emphasis would be placed on economic and foreign relations among nations rather than on cultural or educational exchanges. Quebec would not be given a position at a level comparable to participating heads of state because foreign relations at such a level were considered to be the sole prerogative of the federal government. "Les chefs d'État des pays intéressés veulent rencontrer d'autres chefs d'État et non des dirigeants provinciaux," Mr. Goyer was quoted as saying. (22) The same newspaper reported on October 31 that the French deputy from Loiret, Xavier Deniau, was of the opinion that the proposed commonwealth could not succeed without the participation of France and Quebec.

This series of minor but frequently irritating symbolic trips and events reached a crescendo on November 2, 1977 with the beginning of an official visit to France by Quebec Premier René Lévesque. During his formal three-day tour the Premier was invited to speak to the members of the National Assembly, where his strongly independentist address received a standing ovation. As an indication of France's high regard for Premier Lévesque and his contributions on behalf of French-speaking peoples, President Giscard d'Estaing presented him with the country's highest award, the Legion of Honour medal. This trip was further marked by a formal agreement between France and Quebec to institute regular visits so that the French Premier and the Quebec Premier would be assured of at least yearly opportunities for consultation. Thus, symbolic interchanges have given rise to a formalized provincial foreign policy commitment beyond that which characterizes interactions between officials of the Canadian and French governments.

The events recounted above give some idea of the strained context of federal-Quebec interactions in the sphere of foreign policy. The more the province conducts itself as an incipient state, the less latitude Ottawa wishes to permit Quebec in expressing an international identity. Since the PQ came into office, the atmosphere of Quebec-federal relations appears to have been changing from positive sum to zero sum.

Foreign Policy Intentions

In the event that the Quebec referendum favors independence, the PQ has already begun to develop a foreign policy platform. Early party programs contained statements regarding Québécois solidarity with the Third World, respect for the principle of national self-determination, and other general resolutions. In the 1975 program the PQ proposed the following general measures at the international level: Once an internal referendum has given the government a mandate to declare Quebec a sovereign state, the new country would apply for entry to the United Nations and would seek the recognition of other states. Quebec would respect those treaties made by Canada which it deems to be in its interests. The renunciation of less-favored treaties would be carried out in accord with international law. Efforts would be made to reaffirm and defend the inalienable territory of Quebec, including Labrador, some islands off the coast of Quebec, and part of the present Canadian Arctic. In the event of controversy over these claims,

Quebec proposes to bring its case before an international court of justice. In the economic sphere, the program proposes to establish a customs and monetary union with Canada. Within this context, the terms of the GATT (General Agreement on Tariffs and Trade) and any international legal rulings would be respected in the future elaboration of Quebec's international economic policy. The 1975 program also contains a proviso permitting the creation of a research and supervision body, answerable to the National Assembly, whose aim would be to eliminate political intervention by multi-national corporations in the "State" of Quebec. (23)   However, Premier Lévesque has stated there would be no government take-over of industry with perhaps "one and one-half" exceptions, related to the asbestos industry and automobile insurance. Quebec is the Western world's biggest producer of asbestos fiber.   Although three of the five big companies are American-owned, Quebec wishes to extend its control in order to develop its share of the processing activities. In the area of automobile insurance, a mix of public and private coverage is envisioned. (24)

The 1975 program is more specific regarding other elements of foreign policy such as the intent to respect the principle of non-interference in the internal affairs of other states, and the wish to open a number of diplomatic and consular missions. In a sample 1975-76 budget, tabled by the PQ prior to their election in order to demonstrate how an independent Quebec government would allocate its funds, $26,252,400 was marked for bilateral and multilateral foreign relations, while $44,160,900 was devoted to Quebec aid and development programs. (25)

Most interesting is the priority in which the PQ 1975 platform proposes that an independent Quebec order its international relations. First, relations with the Commonwealth would be replaced by stronger ties with francophone countries.   Second, the establishment of relations with the Third World, particularly Latin America, would be encouraged. Third, priority would be given to establishing close ties linking Quebec to Canada and the United States. (26)

Since the November 1976 election a reassessment of these objectives seems to have been taking place, at least according to newspaper reports. On December 11, 1976 Premier Levesque stated that the most important partners for an independent Quebec were Canada, the United States, "francophonie" (in particular France and Belgium) and the EEC. (27) Later, articles in Le Jour declared that relations with "francophonie" need not exclude preservation of links with the Commonwealth, and one writer even suggests that good relations should be cultivated with belle-mere (mother-in-law) Great Britain. (28) Thus, the priority to be assigned certain countries has been in a state of flux since the victory of the PQ, and the officially proposed order would have to be reevaluated in view of the economic market association which the program also outlined.

The PQ intends to practice a peaceful foreign policy based on "the rejection of warlike methods" as a solution for international differences. It is also committed to disarmament, the interdiction of experimentation with and utilization of nuclear and bacteriological weapons, and the withdrawal from military alliances such as NORAD and NATO. (29) Since 1968 the PQ has attempted to develop its defense policy. In Option Québec, published the same year, Mr. Lévesque proposed that the province's modest forces and military properties, once "repatriated," could be maintained at the cost of $150 million compared with $500 million spent federally as Quebec's share of defense expenditure. (30)   In the mock budget mentioned earlier, the PQ provided for $164,913,000 to finance a force of 8,000 soldiers. (31)

On March 22, 1977 Lévesque was reported as saying that there would be a reconsideration of the party's earlier statements on NATO and NORAD. (32) Even assuming a restrained military posture by an independent Quebec, the Premier suggested that his government might see it as both possible and beneficial to participate in the political and economic aspects of NATO. The extent of PQ participation has not been determined, but certainly the organization constitutes an important source of politico-military information which cannot be ignored.   NORAD was also reconsidered.   The Quebec government appears to recognize its strategic importance for Canada and the United States. Because the PQ wants to establish a customs and monetary union with Canada and have preferential economic relations with the United States, at least minimal cooperation in continental defense is seen as being appropriate. Quebec would integrate to some extent with NORAD, but would unilaterally reject any participation in the existing defense-sharing program. In an interview in U.S. News and World Report, Premier Lévesque stated his clear intention that an independent Quebec would participate in NORAD stating, "That's something we should be part of as long as it didn't ruin us financially. Our doubts would only be about the cost, not the principle, of continental air defense." (33)

It is admitted that PQ foreign policy is incomplete and sometimes contradictory. Pragmatic assessments of Quebec's potential international position have been changing the direction of previous policies since Mr. Lévesque formed his government. On March 4 Le Jour declared that as of November 15, 1976 "the world began to see us as a sovereign country." Such a statement is somewhat premature, given the inherent conservatism of the post-war international community which supports the principle of non-interference in other states' internal affairs. Furthermore, to endorse an independent Quebec state might only serve to legitimate disintegrative ethno-regional movements within long-established states' boundaries.   It appears that the greater effort the PQ government makes to tailor its foreign and defense policies to the realities of the international environment, the more it will find it necessary to moderate its earlier foregn policy statements.

IMPLICATIONS

The birth of foreign policy within sub-regional nationalist movements such as Quebec represents an area of legitimate concern to supra-national bodies such as NATO, NORAD and the European Communities. If many ethno-regional movements were to achieve the success of Quebec in acting in a state-like manner, then the quantitative effect of these movements within the North Atlantic area might begin to make a qualitative difference in existing arrangements.(34) Thus, the tentative foreign policy initiatives being taken by some independentist groups could have significant implications in the larger international context.

At present, ethno-regional movements do not seriously affect the existing North Atlantic defense arrangements. However, attainment of statehood by category three movements could conceivably necessitate a reorganization of current defense relationships. For example, if subjected to sabotage, weakened communication in Quebec could inhibit NATO defense capabilities. The Great Lakes-St. Lawrence basin constitutes a single hydrological system, and is presently divided between two sovereign states and several sub-divisions of each state, being administered cooperatively by the two federal powers. Approximately 1,100 miles of international boundary divides the system. In Canada the St. Lawrence Seaway Authority administers the part of the Seaway owned by the Dominion, controlling assets valued in excess of approximately $500 million, 60% of this amount being the Canadian investment in the St. Lawrence section. The United States counterpart of the Seaway Authority administers assets worth $130 million. (35) If an uncooperative or defenseless Quebec controlled the St. Lawrence portion of the Seaway, this could not only cause trade and communications dislocation in Canada and the United States, it could also block the path of military vessels sailing between the interior and the Atlantic, seriously hampering continental defense capabilities.

Quebec could also prove critical to an energy-starved NATO. In the event of independence, the PQ, Inuit, and Dene would be in a position to decide on the selective distribution of uranium and other mineral resources. It is possible that Europe might attempt to renegotiate a uranium export contract with Quebec. At the present time such a contract is virtually impossible without federal consent, but it is a moot point whether a sovereign Quebec could afford to reject this lucrative international market.

The strength of NATO could be adversely affected by the revival of ethno-regionalism. While the organization is concerned with the instability of new applicants at the state level, it has virtually had to ignore the possible effect which dissident regional movements in major participating countries might have on its continuing viability. This position must remain ambiguous. If NATO takes an overt stand it may exacerbate the problematic situation which exists within any country. Nevertheless, considerations about support for NATO must involve a calculation about the possible multiplier effect of independentist ethno-regional groups. At the very time that the southern flank is weakened by the Turkish-Greek quarrel over Cyprus and Portuguese economic difficulties, the northern flank is faced with significant internal divisions. Ethno-regional conflicts are found throughout the NATO bloc, with language conflicts in Belgium, France, and Norway and the potential for particularly disruptive situations exists in two historically stable NATO members, Canada and Britain. Even in Spain, the only possible new partner for Italy in the creation of a balanced southern NATO, there are major regional and linguistic difficulties.

Within the present context of Canadian involvement in NATO, the territory of Quebec is included in strategic and defense commitments. In the event of independence this involvement would have to be renegotiated, perhaps on terms less favourable to the financial and logistical needs of NATO. The same qualifications would apply to a rearrangement of Quebec's participation in NORAD.

Another difficulty raised by ethno-regional groups is that these may perceive supra-national bodies as alternative political and economic co-ordinating mechanisms capable of replacing existing states. For instance, the desirability of creating a "Europe of Regions" was discussed in August 1976 at a Conference on Regionalism and Decentralization held at Elsinore, Denmark by the Danish Institute. This same organization sponsored a similar conference on the "Europe of Regions" in Copenhagen in September 1977. In Brussels, the Bureau of Unrepresented European Nations lobbies European Community officials regarding ethno-regional interests. Even the PQ has indicated that an independent Quebec would seek to strengthen ties with the European Economic Community.

The European Community has recently undertaken to reconsider treatment of underdeveloped regions within an economic context. However, it appears most unlikely that adjustments to Community regional policy will be reformulated to cope with a disintegrative Europe or North Atlantic area of regions, despite the wishes of some sub-national groups. (36) A European or North Atlantic association of regions would demand considerable alteration of present Community structures. The Commission of the European Communities would become further enmeshed in domestic quarrels over public policy. This is completely counter to its traditional stance which avoids involvement in political interactions which are not immediately related to the creation of the larger European Community.

Even if NATO or the European Community agreed to further specifically regional orientations, such a development would be self-defeating. Ironically, it is the very existence of the present system of military and economic security, painstakingly developed by the North Atlantic states since 1945, which has permitted ethno-regional groups increased maneuverability to pursue their self-interests. Partially because of the success of NATO, NORAD and the European Community, the state is simply no longer seen as the final line of defense against external threats. Rupert Emerson indirectly touched upon this problem when he discussed the nation as a "terminal community - the largest community that, when the chips are down, effectively commands men's loyalty, overriding the claims of both the lesser communities within it and those that cut across it within a still greater society." (37)

It is important that sub-national regionalist groups recognize the necessity of preserving the boundaries of the larger economic and defense communities which initially provided a suitable milieu for the resurgence of within-state protest. Successful independentist groups would have to re-define their viability with reference to a supra-national "terminal" community. However, present foreign policy perspectives of sub-national groups in category three such as Scotland and Quebec, are not reassuring in their firm or effective commitment to a "terminal" North Atlantic entity.

Clearly the phenomenon of ethno-regionalism is not solely the province of harried nation-building states. It has a circular effect on the entire North Atlantic area. Within the context of interdependence, aggregate developments at the sub-national level affect behavior at state and supra-national levels. Because their well-being is affected by ethno-regional foreign policy perspectives and actions, supra-national organizations must consider what policies might be appropriate should any regionalist movements realize their statist goals.   Precedents set in reacting to sub-regional groups in this transitional period will be important to future patterns of sub-supra-national interaction.   For this reason the North Atlantic supra-national community may have to consider abandoning its laissez-faire approach.   It may prove necessary to explain (at least to itself) its interests and to clarify its policy toward those groups which have disintegrative potential.

The state remains the primary area of conflict and major point of reference for present ethno-regional movements.   The conflicting priorities engendered by the interdependent relationship between sub-national and state entities would unlikely be magically resolved by independence.   Major tensions would merely be transferred to other levels, specifically focusing on sub-national and supra-national linkages.   However the universe unfolds, an intelligent appraisal of the foreign policy perspectives of ethno-regional movements is crucial for the constructive adaptation of all actors in the North Atlantic area.

NOTES

(1) Elie Kedourie, Nationalism, 3rd ed. (London: Hutchison, 1966); Cynthia Enloe, Ethnic Conflict and Political Development (Boston: Little, Brown and Company, 1973); Patricia Elton Mayo, The Roots of Identity (London: Allen Lane, 1974); and Theodor Veiter, "The Concept of 'National Minority' and Ethnic Group," Presented at the Conference on Regionalism and Decentralization, The Danish Institute, Elsinore, Denmark, August 1976.

(2) H. J. Hanham, Scottish Nationalism (Cambridge: Harvard University Press, 1969); Nathan Glazer, "The Universalism of Ethnicity," Encounter, September 8-17, 1975; Oriol Pi-Sunyer (ed.), The Limits of Integration: Ethnicity and Nationalism in Modern Europe (Amherst: University of Massachusetts Press, 1971); and James G. Kellas, The Scottish Political System, 2nd ed. (London, New York, Melbourne: Cambridge University Press, 1975).

(3) Walker Connor, "The Politics of Ethnoregionalism," Journal of International Affairs, 27 (1973), pp.1-21; Milton Esman, "Perspectives on Ethnic Conflict in Industrialized Societies," presented at the Conference on Ethnic Pluralism and Conflict in Contemporary Western Europe and Canada, Cornell University, 1975; Glazer, op. cit.; Arend Lijphart, "Ethnic Conflict in the First World: Theoretical Speculations," presented at the Conference on Ethnic Pluralism and Conflict in Contemporary Western Europe and Canada, Cornell University, 1975.

(4) Glazer, op. cit., p. 8; Veiter, op. cit., p. 5

(5) Glazer, op. cit., p. 10.

(6) James N. Rosenau, Linkage Politics, (New York: Free Press, 1969), p. 45.

(7) Ibid., p. 45.

(8) For a discussion of various ways of defining and classifying foreign policy see Charles F. Hermann, "Policy Classification: A Key to the Comparative Study of Foreign Policy," in James N. Rosenau, Vincent Davis,

and Maurice A. East, eds., The Analysis of International Politics (New York, London: The Free Press, 1972), pp. 58-75.

(9) Canadian News Facts, 1977: 1759

(10) Vera Murray, Le Parti Québécois de la fondation à la prise du pouvoir (Montreal: Cahiers du Quebec/HMH Ltee, 1976).

(11) Le Jour, March 4, 1977.

(12) CIDA - Canadian International Development Agency; CUSO - Canadian University Service Overseas.

(13) Louis Sabourin, "Quebec's International Activity Rests on the Idea of Competence," International Perspectives (March/April, 1977), pp. 3-7. See also the collection of articles in Paul Painchaud, ed. Le Canada et le Quebec sur la scène internationale (Montreal: Les Presses de l'Université du Quebec, 1977).

(14) Ibid., p. 6; and Claude Morin, Quebec versus Ottawa: The Struggle for Self-government 1960-72. Translated from "Le Pouvoir québécois... en negociation" and "Le Combat québécois" by Richard Howard (Toronto: University of Toronto Press, 1972 and 1973).

(15) Morin, op. cit., p. 40.

(16) Ibid., p. 42.

(17) Paul Martin, Secretary of State for External Affairs, Federalism and International Relations (Ottawa: Queen's Printer, 1968), p. 25.

(18) Denis Stairs, "Devolution and Foreign Policy: Prospects and Possibilities," Presented at the Conference on the Future of Canadian Confederation, University of Toronto, October 14-15, 1977, p. 36.

(19) The Montreal Star, July 26, 1977.

(20) Journal de Montreal, July 26, 1977.

(21) Globe & Mail, July 28, 1977.

(22) Le Devoir, October 26, 1977.

(23) Parti Québécois, Le Programme du Parti Québécois (Montreal: Editions du Parti Québécois, 1975), pp. 5, 10, 17-18.

(24) U.S. News and World Report, September 26, 1977, p. 72.

(25) Parti Québécois, Premier Budget d'un Quebec Indépendant. Exercice financier 1975-1976 (Project) (Montreal: Editions du Parti, Québécois, 1973), Section 3-1 to 3-5.

(26) Parti Québécois, op. cit., 1975, p. 9.

(27) Le Jour, May 27, 1977.

(28) Le Jour, May 20, 1977.

(29) Parti Québécois, op. cit., 1975, p. 9.

(30) René Lévesque, An Option for Quebec, English translation of "Option Quebec," (Toronto and Montreal: McClelland & Stewart, Ltd., 1968), p. 50.

(31) Parti Québécois, op. cit. 1975, Section 11-3.

(32) Le Jour, May 27, 1977.

(33) U.S. News and World Report, September 26, 1977, p. 71.

(34) Walker Connor, "Nationbuilding or Nation-Destroying?" World Politics, 24 (April, 1972), p. 330.

(35) F.J.E. Jordan, "Sharing the Seaway System," in One Country or Two? R. M. Burns, ed. (Montreal and London: McGill-Queen's University Press, 1971), pp. 98, 103.

(36) Commission of the European Communities, Guidelines for Community Regional Policy (Brussels), June 1977, pp. 21-22.

(37) Rupert Emerson, From Empire to Nation (Cambridge: Harvard University Press, 1960), pp. 95-96.

8 Quebec Nationalism: Some Levels of Socio-Political Analysis
Panayotis Soldatos*

INTRODUCTION

The aim of this chapter is to provide an inventory which, although not exhaustive at its levels of analysis, may facilitate systematic relection about the present dimensions of Quebec nationalism and enable us to delimit its essential socio-political framework. In addition, the relations between this nationalism and certain basic orientations of contemporary nationalism will be considered.

The complexity of the national question in Quebec requires some introductory observations about the empirical aspects of our approach and the essence of this particular nationalism.

From the empirical point of view, we are aware of the dangers which beset any attempt at reflection on current burning issues in which the images of the protagonists comprise, besides their cognitive dimension, an affective, not to say emotional, dimension and a strong tendency to socio-political action. (1) We shall, thus, try to distinguish political analysis from politics itself in order to preserve the necessary freedom of explanation, without being able, nor desiring, to postulate a perfect neutrality, since as investigators we ourselves belong to the historical and social circumstances which we are observing.

On the conceptual side, we shall not attempt a systematic exegesis of the definition of Quebec nationalism for several reasons. The limits of our exposition, which constitutes a small part of this more extensive, collective book, preclude such an attempt. As we deal here with an all-embracing and succinct reflection, it is possible, for the purpose of the analysis, to define Quebec nationalism from its basic underlying aims in an empirico-descriptive manner. Our observations on the various levels of analysis of the phenomenon

* The author of this study wishes to thank Miss Miren A. Letemendia, research assistant at CEDE, for her help with the English version of this text.

suffice to suggest certain basic characteristics of Quebec nationalism and to indicate the outlines of a definition.

Having stated this, we find, when it comes to identifying the hard core of Quebec nationalism, a body of attitudes and behaviors, engaged or permissive, precise or diffuse. These are accompanied by a will or a desire with several components: the need to affirm a feeling of collective belonging ("We-feeling," "sense of community"), to preserve an ethnic, cultural, social heritage, to promote a collective creativity in socio-cultural matters (defensive ethno-nationalism), to acquire a much larger range of powers in the perspective of increased national or regional autonomy (nationalism vs. sub-national regionalism), and finally, to favor accelerated economic development and social peace within the frame of a nation-state (New Nationalism of a welfare state).

This nationalism also has external ramifications and orientations (outward-looking nationalism). Quebec, in the 1960s, for reasons of internal politics and external affiliations, had to pass from provincialism to internationalism (2) almost without transition, thereby opening itself up to a vast constellation of protagonists in the international system: relations with France and French-speaking countries in general, ties with the United States, relationships with the countries of Latin America, and interests in the European Community.

PROPOSED EIGHT LEVELS OF ANALYSIS

After these introductory observations concerning the orientation and delimitation of the subject, we pass to the central part of our approach. We shall propose certain levels of analysis, which together could provide a framework for the general study of Quebec nationalism and identify certain elements of its essential socio-political essence.

The levels of analysis set out below are based on a consideration of certain situational elements of the Quebec and Canadian systemic milieu of environmental factors which are extra-systemic to the said nationalism, and of the attitudes and behavior of the actors who express the national ideal in Quebec. Needless to say, in an attempt to select and synthesize, we shall have to limit ourselves here to some levels of reflection which reveal the essence of Quebec nationalism and situate it in relation to other forms of nationalism - Third World nationalism characterized by increased acquisition of an ideology, radicalization, and armed struggle and nationalism of an essentially socio-economic character which is found particularly in developed countries (New Nationalism).

The Level of the Public Institutional Machinery

Within the framework of participation in the federal type of government, Quebec society has witnessed, in an atmosphere of conflict, the development of a number of provincial institutions of which the organic form and functional activity, in qualitative terms, are not too far removed from those of political systems of the type seen in modern states, with the exclusion of defense. (3) After the arrival in power of the <u>Parti Québécois,</u> this government machinery has served as a pivot to the nationalist movement. It is a guarantee, in the view of the _Parti_, of a possible transformation of the system (the creation of a Quebec sovereign state out of the present provincial state) without functional disruption and other interruptions.

Consequently, the relationship between Quebec nationalism and public institutions becomes a relationship which necessarily influences the national evolution of Quebec society, in accordance with the relation "Nation-State (provincial) - Nation-State (sovereign)."

The Level of the Elites

The existence of effects of interaction and retroaction, linking the development of a political system to its elites, is not to be disregarded. To cite only a very general instance, the phenomena of modernization of Quebec have a definite impact on Quebec elites who, in their turn, do not fail to condition the systemic development of their society.

Thus, the presence of an elite in Quebec, whose functional capacities cover a wide range of issue-areas normally included in a political system of the type of modern states, is linked to the causes and effects of systemic modernization, and, in this capacity, does not fail to have an influence on the future of a collectivity (Quebec) which has a project of national emancipation.

This impact is, in our view, twofold. On the one hand, the Quebec elite, conscious of its partly unused technocratic capacity and the restrictions of the Quebec system (limited internal and embryonic external state competences, weak participation of French-speaking elites in key positions in the economic sector of Quebec, rivalry within the system between French and English-speaking elites) can only stimulate Quebec nationalism with a view to creating a system disposing of greater scope of function, both qualitative and quantitative. On the other hand, the presence of an elite accelerates, voluntarily or involuntarily, the process of national emancipation by creating an atmosphere of security, thanks to the certainty it offers the population that in the event of the creation of a sovereign state unity in Quebec, the continuity of the systemic activities of a new, enlarged political process can be insured.

The Level of the Collective Structures

In addition to its multi-dimensional elite and its government structures, Quebec has been able to acquire progressively a number of organizations for collective action which are destined to increase, thus permitting it to anticipate, in case of a break in the federal link, a certain stability in the system. These represent a gamut of institutional groups, such as the political parties, (4) the economic organizations of public utility, the various Quebec companies of significant size, the pressure groups, the caisses populaires, the consumers' and producers' cooperatives, the school organizations, the religious groups, the units of mass media, and the socio-cultural associations in general.

As far as their functions within the system are concerned, those that are favorable to Quebec nationalism are many-sided: functions such as mere grouping, socialization, participation, revindication, selection of political personnel, accumulation of socio-economic powers.

The Level of the Links of Social Communication

The participation of Quebec in the federal system, as well as its key position in the Canadian geo-political space, has led Quebec society to develop ties of socio-political communication with the whole of Canada. Without disregarding the fact that this integration is imperfect and asymmetrical, from a comparative and deontological point of view - reference being made to the relationships with each of the Canadian provinces - it can be stated that the elite and the masses of Quebec fit into a schema of double-belonging and loyalism linking them to the federal political superstructure as well as to that of their Province. Conflicts of allegiance are created because of the mobility between one level of government and another, and those French-speaking elites who have chosen to operate in the federal government are sometimes assimilated into it, especially on the socio-political and administrative levels.

This process of communication within the system frequently deprives Quebec of the services of some of its leaders and elites who work at the federal level and who, in the end, constitute opposition to those of the Province, and, in particular, to Quebec nationalist elites.

The Level of the Systemic Development

The four levels of analysis which we have identified above indicate certain socio-political and technocratic elements of the development of the Quebec system. However, the sub-stratum of this development is larger, extending in particular to the economic sphere, and is measured by various indicators (GNP, GNP per capita, industrialization, distribution of tasks within the active population, diversification of economic activities, foreign exchanges, urbanization, to name some).

Thus, without neglecting the burden of regional differences which weighs fairly heavily on Quebec society, we may consider that Quebec nationalism is developing within a sophisticated political community which belongs to the group of so-called developed countries. This explains, together of course with other variables, the moderation of the Quebec nationalist movement (5) which tries to convince the population of Quebec of the viability, in economic terms, of the independence option, and to avoid, in the choice of its means of action, irreparably disturbing the systemic working of Quebec and its political process. The more advanced the society in terms of systemic development (socio-political and economic), the more it produces conservative political attitudes and methods and in means, dissuades national movements from the path of radicalization in national emancipation. The debate on the first budget of Quebec as a sovereign state, the formula of one or several referenda, and, in short, the attachment of supporters of Quebec independence to the political procedures of Western democracies are largely due to the degree of development of Quebec society.

The Level of the External Systemic Links

Quebec society is closely linked, by inter-governmental and trans-national relationships, to the global international system, which is divided into Center and Periphery zones.   Because of its standard of living and its regular relationships - due to the dynamics within the continent - with the core area of the Center, the United States, Quebec represents a country of the Center. However, as a country with strong regional differences, as one with a capacity to produce raw materials but without an autonomous and satis-factory degree of industrialization to manufacture finished products, and as one threatened by the American cultural influence, it has certain ties to the Third World (French-speaking countries, etc.) which draw it to the Periphery (mixed characteristics of industrialized and Third World countries.)   Thus, it appears that the evolution of the process of national independence will also depend on the positions which external protagonists - especially those of the Center, and particularly the United States - will adopt on the matter, on Quebec's understanding of these positions, and on the perception, be it correct or false, which the Quebec protagonists have and will have of their position within the international system.

On the ethnic and cultural level, Quebec is a national community without a region or a hinterland.   Whereas most nationalisms form part of a larger surrounding and contiguous family (in particular, international sub-systems), characterized by a solidarity based on race, geo-politics and religion (Arab nationalism and the Arab world, African nationalism and Black culture, South-East Asia as a systemic area, etc.), Quebec is at a considerable distance from the French-speaking world and cannot find a contiguous supporting system in the context of the North American sub-continent.

In addition, this situation creates a certain ambivalence in the attitude of the French-speaking elite of Quebec, who are subject to the pressure of geographical gravity (the attraction of the United States "border syndrome") and of ethnic and cultural forces (the attraction of France).

The Level of the Objectives

On the level of the objectives, Quebec nationalism in the 1970s is marked by very diverse colorings, according to the political elite who are its spokesmen. From the sub-national regionalism of the Liberal Party to the integral nationalism of the Parti Québécois, through the egalitarian federalism of the Union Nationale, we find a whole range of orientations which necessitate the use of a variety of concepts of sometimes arduous scientific precision. It is, however, clear that on the basis of the goals of Quebec nationalism it is possible to identify the outlines of a national reality which is multi-dimensional. Hence, a definition of Quebec nationalism cannot be univocal and must integrate the various objectives of the movement.

The Level of the Determinants

We must now deal with a lengthy list of many-sided causes. Besides the general cultural and national aspirations of the Québécois (elites and masses), there are the more economic motivations of a community which reacts to intra-systemic and extra-systemic economic stresses and adopts policies of New Nationalism. Confronted with the highly complex interplay of trans-national forces (in particular, the multi-nationals) which accelerate the internationalization of production and threaten the small and medium-sized companies and the weak sectors of the Quebec economy, confronted with the pressures of a public in socio-economic disarray demanding increased intervention by the government as protagonist of the welfare state, confronted with the functional incapacity of the national economic circles to cope in the face of the harsh international competition of today, many Quebec leaders and private individuals are led to try to accentuate the control of the political and economic system and to claim new powers of action.

FINAL CONSIDERATIONS

From this brief outline of some of the levels of analysis of Quebec nationalism, it appears that this multi-dimensional phenomenon resembles several types of traditional and contemporary nationalism, which we shall recapitulate here.

On the level of objectives, Quebec nationalism takes several forms. It is a traditional nationalism, based on the principle of nationalities, common to developed countries as well as to those of the Third World. It is also a New Nationalism with socio-economic characteristics representing the desire of provincial state powers to control more strongly an economy which is shaken by trans-national currents, the internationalization of production, the international division of labor and international competition, and to answer the demand of a population at grips with inflation and unemployment. It is also a sub-national regionalism for those who hope to increase the powers of the state of Quebec while remaining within the federal schema (egalitarian or non-egalitarian). Finally, it is an ethno-cultural nationalism protecting Quebec's cultural sovereignty.

On the level of the means, Quebec nationalism has the characteristics of a moderate nationalism which is "non-ideologized" (6) and acts within the framework of the democratic lines of a developed society. In general, one does not find here the radicalization of ideology of the nationalist movements in the Third World which often goes hand in hand with armed conflictive situations.

In addition, the framework of a developed society, within which the Quebec process of national awakening and revindication is taking place, affects the rhythm of promotion of the theses of the national question. Situated in a country which is economically dominated, although relatively prosperous, the population of Quebec cannot make a purely political and cultural choice about the national question, but must consider the economic and social repercussions of national emancipation. Hence there is the need for a solid economic argument (budget of an independent Quebec, etc.) to ease the hesitation of certain sectors of the population who, when faced with the possibility of auto-determination and the breaking of the federal link, fear a disturbance in the mechanisms of the socio-economic life. Once again, the difference with the situations of nationalism in the Third World are fairly marked.

Placed within a schema of Center-Periphery, the elites and the population of Quebec are conscious of the limits along the path to emancipation, and realize the very restrictive lines of a political or, better still, a juridico-institutional independence. The economic weight of the external protagonists and the United States in particular can only continue to mark the economic life of Quebec and would perpetuate and, according to some, increase, its links of economic dependence, thus conferring a nominal character on political independence. These statements somewhat reduce the nationalist ardor of certain people, whereas they provoke others into wishing to ideologize the process and to advocate political independence accompanied by a change in values, in regime, and in type of society.

It is again this dependence which permits some to forecast that the foreign policy of an independent Quebec will not be able to stray beyond the orientations of that of Canada, a country within the Center-Periphery frame and with a network of asymmetrical, unfavorable links with the United States (7).

Quebec is characterized by a nationalism which is inward-looking as regards its objectives, and outward-looking as to its means.   Cut off geographically from its cultural and ethnic sources, and possessing the economic gauge of a small power, it realizes the need for an active foreign policy of association in almost every direction, and for a formula of continental integration with the rest of Canada. In this regard, we note the rare combination of a nationalist project of political independence together with a political project of international integration.

Starting from the sphere of low politics the action of the nationalist elites of Quebec has contributed to the politicization of the Federal provincial dialogue to the domestication of foreign policy activities subjecting them to internal priorities, and to the abolition of barriers between high politics and low politics.

Unlike the processes used by the Third World countries in their bids for national independence, consisting of a claim for decolonization "pure and simple" and giving rise to a zero-sum game, the case of Quebec nationalism, bearing elements of association and accommodation with English Canada, is oriented toward the more subtle options of a non-zero-sum game.

These considerations are bound to be limited inasmuch as our approach is only an attempt at a general, all-embracing, preliminary study. It is aimed at stimulating thought, and is not intended either to exhaust the possible levels of analysis or to propose definitive answers to a topical question, which is determined by numerous intra-systemic and extra-systemic variables.

NOTES

(1) For this conceptualization of the term "image," see R.B. Byers, D. Leyton-Brown, Peyton V. Lyon, "The Canadian International Image Study," in International Journal, 1977, no. 3, p. 605.

(2) The statement is by G. Bergeron.

(3) It must be emphasized that this politico-administrative superstructure covers not only the domain of systemic internal activities, but also the field of foreign relations: in foreign relations, Quebec already disposes of information structures, structures of management analysis, of coordination and of representation (see P. Painchaud, "Le role international du Quebec: Possibilités et contraintes," in Etudes interationales, 1977, no. 2, p. 381).

(4) The organization of the Parti Québécois, in particular, is an example of a modern party incorporating the masses (adhesion, organization of militants, financing, dialogue with the "deputés" and the ministers belonging to the Parti, etc.).

(5) Moderation in political aims and methods of action.

(6) Moreover, the national question has, up to a certain point, hindered the development in Quebec of an ideological debate on the foundations of the regime and of the society.

(7) P. Painchaud, op. cit., develops the various foreign policy choices of an independent Quebec.

9 Sub-National Regionalism or Sub-State Nationalism: The Irish Case
J. J. Lee

It will perhaps avoid misunderstanding with respect to the Irish dimension of the subject if I state clearly that the term "sub-national regionalism" does not strike me as completely satisfactory. It begs the question. Regionalism tends to carry pejorative connotations suggesting a kind of impatience at the persistence of a primitive political faith whose devotees should really know better by now and resign themselves to the inevitable march of history. This paper will avoid the term, and substitute, at least in the Irish context, the more historically accurate and emotionally neutral term, "sub-state nationalism." I regard nationalism as a purely subjective feeling, a political sentiment based on a shared sense of nationality. If a group of people feel that they constitute a nationality, then they constitute a nationality. If they do not, then they do not, even if they appear to possess all the marks of true nationality so lovingly listed by students of the phenomenon. Whether a nationalist movement succeeds in achieving political expression in a national state depends largely on historical and demographic circumstances, and, of course, on the circumstance of what other nationalist movements may have rival claims on the same territory. Too many nationalities chasing too few territories lead to sub-state nationalism. "Majority" and "minority," the alpha and omega of democratic right and wrong within homogenous communities are meaningless terms in the context, because the valid unit of reference is the nationality itself. In practical political terms, a scattered minority, however intense its subjective feeling of nationality, can hardly punch its political weight, and can largely be politically discounted for our purposes. A demographically concentrated minority, on the other hand, can, if it wishes, draft a different political script. Four million nationalist Irishmen scattered throughout the United Kingdom in 1920 would not have constituted a political problem. Concentrated in Ireland, they did. One million Protestants scattered throughout Ireland would not today constitute a serious political problem, at least from the point of view of posing a threat to the country's territorial integrity. Concentrated in North-East Ulster, they do. Even a half-million Catholics scattered among one million Ulster Protestants, roughly the present Northern Irish situation, would not constitute a serious menace to the security of the Northern State. Heavily concentrated, as most of them are, in urban ghettos and rural clusters, they can pose a constant threat in Ulster.

These crude observations may help us understand the Irish, and more particularly the Ulster, situation. The Ulster question revolves around an old-fashioned racial struggle. The attitude of the Protestant people of Ulster toward the Catholic people of Ulster seems to me to be predominately racist. The Catholic attitude toward Protestants, though distinctly less racist, seems to be at least tinged with more racism than is Irish nationalism in general, which remains relatively free from racism. Some scholars would regard this description as a crude over-simplification. I only wish it were. It may be true that the racial image which the Ulster Protestant cherishes of Catholics may reveal some confusion behind the stereotype. (1) This itself reflects the primacy of the racial imperative, when in fact incompatible and illogical combinations of responses are huddled together under the same umbrella, however leaky.

The racist attitude appears to have already existed on the part of the settler race. There may have been some crossing of the ethnic frontier, at least from the native to the planter community, in the seventeenth century settlement. This was probably inevitable, if only because of the unbalanced sex ratio of the settler community. However there is little evidence of much crossing of the boundaries in the past century. Today segregation in Northern Ireland is more rampant than it is between black and white in the United States. The residential segregation index is extremely high. Education below the university level is almost completely segregated. Marriage takes place virtually exclusively within the two racial communities, whose boundaries are defined by religious criteria. Religion, in turn, is a convenient shorthand definition of racial loyalty rather than a theological system. "Catholic" and "Protestant" summarize the bundle of predominant ascriptive prejudices, just as do "black" and "white" in more familiar racial situations. As life in general revolves around kinship relations, not only in rural areas, but also in urban ones - Ulster towns are largely groupings of "the village in the city" - marriage within the one community effectively confines the overwhelming bulk of one's life contacts to members of one's own community. Tradition-ally, outsiders have great difficulty in understanding Ulster. However, they probably know more about the two communities than either Ulster community knows about the other.

This communal antipathy has existed for three centuries. The struggle has assumed a new intensity during the past decade, however, due to several factors. Above all, a new leadership cadre of educated laity has emerged on the hitherto submerged Catholic side. Previous Catholic political movements have tended to be dominated by the clergy who were essentially conservative and generally rather badly educated - even if better educated than the average member of their flock - and whose intentions centered on limited practical gains rather than on civil rights. The educational reforms embodied in the Butler Act of 1944 created a new style of Catholic leadership, personified in the younger generation who overthrew the old nationalist party and, in 1970, established the new Social Democratic and Labor Party. The old

Catholic leadership had to be superseded before the Protestant supremacy could be challenged. It is a recurring liberal illusion that education eliminates local loyalties, and enables the educated to transcend their ancestral regional heritage. This may indeed happen when the legitimacy of the State is generally accepted. Where it is not, education merely sharpens the appreciation of, and articulation of, resentment against the establishment. Discrimination against Catholic professional people, against potential Catholic applicants for the public service did not become a major political problem as long as relatively few Catholics with generally mediocre education were involved. (2) When a generation at last emerged which felt itself to be, and in many respects was, at least as well educated as the favored Protestant appointees, resentment boiled over and found more effective expression than hitherto. If the continuing horror of the para-military conflict reflects the improved leadership of the I.R.A., the continuance of the constitutional political struggle reflects above all the calibre of a new Catholic political leadership which has improved out of all recognition. That is one reason why the present crisis has continued for so long, and will continue indefinitely. It is no longer merely a round of riots, played out in a season, or even a climactic civil war situation of 1920-22 vintage. It is now an on-going situation. The rise of this type of leadership may be a prime reason for the discontent of sub-state nationalities throughout the world. The sheer contempt for the incompetence of government, the conviction of the educated elites that they couldn't possibly make a bigger mess of things themselves has fueled the fires of "Regional" resentment with lethal doses of intellectual and aesthetic contempt for the central government.

There is no obvious solution in sight to the Ulster question. It may be that a peace of exhaustion will set in, but this is highly unlikely. With the advance in guerilla technology, a very small number of technically skilled men can inflict vast destruction on life and property. Regular claims of the British military, or of opportunist British politicians that the crisis is on the verge of solution, can be discounted. The problem is that while every group involved - whether the Protestant or the Catholic para-militaries, the British or the Irish governments - can veto an uncongenial solution, none of them is strong enough to impose his own solution. As long as the racial issue predominates it is difficult to visualize any enduring solution, which must, short of genocide, be based on good will. Above all, it is the racial imperative which prevents a settlement; virtually all the specific issues can be settled on the basis of already existing proposals by the Irish and British governments. As long as visceral racial reactions dominate the Protestant people, there is no way they will voluntarily agree to accept a situation where they are not "cocks of the Ulster walk."

The Ulster question cannot be treated in isolation from either the Irish or the British dimensions. The Catholic people of Ulster, however proud of their specific Ulster qualities, identify overwhelmingly, at least in the abstract, with Irish nationalism. They both are, and see themselves as, the object of Irish irredentist aspiration. They identify with the biggest nationality within Ireland. The Protestant people of Ulster, on the other hand, have a much more articulated sense of racial identity than the majority of English, Scots, or Welsh, though they may be somewhat confused as to which precise racial identity it is. However, that is commonly the case with settler peoples. The Ulster planters are perhaps a race in search of a nation, perhaps even in search of a nation-state. If it were not for their geographical proximity to Britain they would in all likelihood have already developed their own brand of nationalism, as distinct from nationality. Suffice it to say that one cannot ignore the British and Irish dimensions, if only because the problem would be quite different if Britain and Ireland did not exist. If the Protestant people of Ulster did not feel a particular affinity for Britain, and if the Catholic people of Ulster did not feel a particular affinity for the Republic of Ireland there might still be an Ulster problem, but it would be a quite different Ulster problem from the present one and the options open to the conflicting communities would be significantly different. The extreme Irish nationalist pretense that Britain should not be involved in any way, and the extreme British nationalist pretense that Ireland should not be involved in any way provide a recipe for continuing conflict, and postpone the possibility of any enduring solution.

The Atlantic implications of the Ulster question have so far been strangely muted. It seems clear that the I.R.A. relied heavily in the early 1970s on Irish-American money, which was sometimes used to procure Soviet-type weapons. The flow of American funds appears to have declined following the energetic efforts of the Irish government to impress on Irish-Americans that the Northern Irish situation is much more complex than the traditional Irish-American version of Irish history assumes. The Irish government, however, cannot dissuade opportunistic American politicians angling for the Irish-American vote from patronizing a particular interpretation of Irish history, though it can belatedly attempt to educate Irish-Americans to a more mature perspective on both the Irish past and the Irish present.

Direct Soviet involvement in the North Irish imbroglio would appear to be minimal, despite the efforts of some more extreme Unionists to flagellate themselves into a frenzy of excitement about the matter. Northern Ireland, no less than Ireland as a whole, must remain the despair of Marxist tacticians as well as theorists. Nevertheless, continuing instability, probably inevitable as long as British troops remain, cannot be in the interest of the Atlantic community even if it offers little immediate prospects of increased Soviet influence in the area.

The Ulster question, like the Irish question in general, has been handled by most English politicians and administrators with a degree of ineptness exceeded only by that of their military advisors. The experience gained by the British army in counter-insurgency techniques, which some observers count as an important advantage in their present involvement, has borne singularly little fruit in the conflict itself. Its relevance to other conceivable types of guerrilla campaigns in the United Kingdom in the foreseeable future seems debatable. The real military lesson of the Ulster troubles is that a relatively small group of activists can sustain a struggle indefinitely if they enjoy even the passive support of concentrated enclave opinion. This they can maintain virtually at will by escalating the conflict and polarizing the situation whenever circumstances demand it. Anglo-Irish relations remain to some extent at the mercy of small groups of extremists as long as the Ulster imbroglio continues.   It seems unlikely that any Irish government could contemplate entering NATO, or even an alternative Western European defense system, as long as British troops remain in Northern Ireland.   The wider strategic implications of either an independent Northern Ireland, or of a united Ireland no longer clinging to military neutralism have received little public attention, though it is not inconceivable that they may assume increasing importance.   Indeed, it is possible that the general gains from a solution to the problem would repay a higher intellectual investment in the Ulster question on the part of those most concerned with the future of Atlantic relations.

NOTES

(1)   Some serious students, like Conor Cruise O'Brien "Northern Ireland: Its Past and Its Future; the Future", RACE, XIV, 1, 1972 and S. Nelson, "Protestant Ideology Considered: A Case of 'Discrimination'" in I. Crew (Ed.), British Political Sociology Notebook, 2, (London, 1975) reject the "racial" interpretation of Ulster history, on the grounds either that there is no objective difference between the races, or that Protestants do not attribute ascriptively racial qualities to Catholics.   But the fact remains that Ulster Protestants have long thought in racial categories about Catholics.

(2)   Edmund A. Aunger, "Religion and Occupational Class in Northern Ireland," Economic and Social Review, 7, 1, 1975, provides the most authoritative study of socio-economic structure by religious classification. D. Donnison, "The Northern Ireland Civil Service," New Society, 5 July, 1973, p.8, notes that in 1972 95% of four hundred and seventy-seven senior civil servants in Northern Ireland were Protestants.

10 Trans-National Policy in a Sub-Regional Context: The Case of Scotland

Charles R. Foster *

The spectacular electoral gains of the Scottish Nationalist Party (SNP) over the last decade have suddenly attracted much attention to the historic Scottish claim for autonomy in the United Kingdom. Standard textbooks on British politics have not mentioned the existence of nationalist movements in Britain. (1) Nevertheless, nationalism has had a long-term position in Scotland. It has been sustained by various institutions such as the Church of Scotland, Scots law, and a separate local government system, as well as by a host of informal institutions including the Scottish Opera, Scottish football, and Scottish trade unions. These institutions help keep alive the historical differences between the Scots and the English, and they provide bases around which political identification coalesces.

Having polled approximately 2.4% of the Scottish vote in 1964, the SNP more than doubled its share in 1966 when it received 5.4% of the Scottish vote. After having won its first seat in Parliament in 1967, the Party came away from the February 1974 General Election with seven seats and 21.9% of the Scottish vote. Finally, in the October 1974 General Election, the first election in which it contested all 71 Scottish seats, the SNP captured 11 of them and increased its share of the vote to 30.4%. At the same time, due to the gerrymandering of the British constituencies, the Conservative Party secured the 16 Scottish seats with only 25% of the total vote.

Some observers attributed the SNP's initial success at the polls to "protest voting"; others have since attributed it to the Scots' unwillingness to share forthcoming North Sea oil reserves with the rest of Britain. However, the SNP acquired considerable support before the extent of the North Sea oil reserves was known; and the party's voting strength is now substantially beyond the level which could be ascribed to "protest voting."

* The author gratefully acknowledges the research assistance of Mary Elizabeth Kehler, a graduate student at the School of Advanced International Studies, Johns Hopkins University.

Various opinion polls in 1977 indicate that the SNP continues to command more support than any other party. Both the election data and the poll data indicate that, unlike the Mouvement Poujadiste, Scottish national-ism is here to stay. (2)

Scottish nationalism is not, in fact, a new phenomenon. Since 1707, when the Act of Union joined the two nations of England and Scotland, the Scots have managed to preserve and develop a distinctive culture and society, despite England's predominance in almost every sphere of activity. The terms of the union protected the Church of Scotland, Scots Law, and Scottish education, thereby preserving the major institutions of Scottish life. Although the number of Gaelic-speakers has steadily diminished (there is no language issue in Scotland), Scotland does have a strong literary tradition of which its people are very proud.

In part, the SNP derives its support from this sense of cultural identity which the Scots have been able to retain throughout Scotland's union with England. (3) The SNP's sudden surge of new strength, however, is primarily due to an accumulation of Scottish economic dissatisfactions. One of the chief reasons the Scottish elite agreed to the Act of Union in 1707 was that association with England during the period of colonial expansion offered economic opportunities to the upper and middle classes which would not otherwise have been available. Indeed, trade with British colonies and free access to the English market gave Scots new outlets for their talents and energies and brought Scotland a degree of prosperity it had not known before.

Fluctuations in Scotland's level of economic activity have generally paralleled those in England, Scotland's major market. As long as the English economy was expanding, Scotland flourished. When England entered a period of economic stagnation after World War I, the Scottish economy declined as well. During the inter-war years, when England suffered, first from poor economic and fiscal policies and then from depression, insufficient invest-ments were made in Scotland's principal industries: coal, steel, shipbuilding, and heavy engineering. World War II offered Scotland a brief respite. The demand for Scottish industrial products increased, and the wartime industrial-dispersal policy led to the introduction of new technologically sophisticated industry. However, after the initial boom of post-war reconstruction and a short period of full employment, the Scottish economy was still heavily reliant on a few obsolete heavy industries unable to diversify and restructure rapidly. In 1955, Scotland entered a period of economic decline from which it has never fully recovered.

Clearly, the favorable economic conditions which originally made union with England seem attractive to the Scots no longer exist. Moreover, as prevailing conditions in the world economy have changed, it is increasingly doubtful in the minds of many Scots whether the advantages of union with England still outweigh the disadvantages. Although Scotland has had its own difficulties in attracting foreign investment, due to its remoteness from many markets and its reputation for militant labor, London's initial failure to join the European Community deprived Scotland of new industry eager to penetrate the Common External Tariff of the Six. In addition, given the general trend toward economic centralization, decisions affecting the Scottish economy tend to be made in corporate headquarters in London according to the needs of British or multi-national firms; and these decisions are not necessarily in the interest of Scotland. Scotland also appears to be losing much of its entrepreneurial talent to London, as it is increasingly true that positions of responsibility are only to be obtained outside of Scotland. (4)

Beyond these economic dissatisfactions, two other phenomena have also caused Scots to question their relationship with England. Both of these can be found in a number of other ethnic conflict situations in post-industrial societes.

The first is the reaction against the modern trend toward centralized, over-loaded government. The distant London bureaucracy is ill-suited to satisfy Scottish needs, and there is a feeling that Scottish affairs should be directed from Scotland. The civil servants who oversee the daily adminis- tration of Scottish affairs are part of the central Civil Service whose first loyalty is to London.

The second of these phenomena is a need to identify with a group, the need to "belong." (5) This is a reaction against the dissolution of family and village life brought on by the increased mobility, education, and communi- cation which characterizes modern society. At a time when other groups have lost their cohesiveness and individuals have an increasing sense of rootlessness and unimportance, the Scottish nationalist movement has given Scots a new sense of identification. Although Scottish nationalism, like nationalism in other countries, developed in reaction to economic and political ideas which initially had little relation to traditionalism, the recent search for roots has helped the movement gain momentum. (6) Supporting the SNP and its calls for an altered relationship with England appears to be a logical consequence of these ideas.

The main demand of the SNP has been Scottish independence, an independence to be achieved by democratic electoral methods. The party, however, concentrates on specific issues and talks little about independence. The issues run from pension rights to natural resource conservation, from land-use planning to opposition to British entry into the European Community. The party doctrine is moderately social-democratic and is designed to appeal to middle-class people.   In fact the Labour Government regarded the increasing strength of the SNP in 1968 municipal elections as a demand for home rule. (7) In 1969 it appointed a Royal Commission on the Constitution whose report, known as the Kilbrandon Report (after its second Chairman, Scottish Law Lord Kilbrandon), was released in 1973.

The recommendations of the Kilbrandon Report included broad executive and legislative powers for Scotland. It gave non-partisan respectability to the cause of devolution. A special Labour Party conference was held in Glasglow on August 17, 1974 which endorsed a Scottish Assembly. This cleared the way for a Government White Paper in September 1974 (8) which committed the Labour Government to the establishment of Scottish and Welsh Assemblies. A second, more detailed White Paper was issued in November 1975 (9) with proposals that were fiercely attacked in Scotland as too restrictive.   It included very weak taxation and economic powers, and did not establish a separate Scottish Civil Service. Worst of all, from the Scottish point of view, it included veto and supervisory powers for the UK Parliament and the Secretary of State for Scotland.

A third White Paper (10) issued in November 1976 made some minor changes to strengthen the Assembly's powers. The Scotland and Wales Bill was introduced on November 29, 1976 and passed its Second Reading on December 17, 1976, at which time the government promised a referendum in Scotland and Wales. This was a massive document of 166 pages containing 115 clauses. Given the larger number of amendments that were offered, the Government was forced to move a 20 day "guillotine," a parliamentary measure to limit the time that can be spent on the different parts of the proposed legislation. The motion failed by 29 votes on February 22, 1977, thus, in effect, killing the bill. Labour discontent, Conservative solidarity, and Liberal insistence on its unique devolution views killed the bill, which was formally abandoned in June 1977.

In the fall of 1977 the government introduced a new Scottish devolution bill containing a referendum provision. Recently the bill has been weakened by two new requirements: first, that it be approved by 40% of the total electorate, and second, that it exclude the Shetland and Orkney Islands from the proposed devolution plan. The first change will make an abstention in the devolution referendum a vote against devolution. The second change would force Scotland to share part of its oil reserves with the Shetland Islands. (11) It is evident from the current Commons debate on the devolution bill that, although it will set up a Scottish Assembly in Edinburgh, it will not satisfy the Scottish nationalists.

In an early Commons debate on devolution in January 1975, SNP member George Reid said: "The aim of my party is clear. It is the restoration of national sovereignty to the people of Scotland and, ultimately, the withdrawal of all Scottish members from this House.... Devolution is not a once-for-all, immutable transfer of powers, but a continuing and on-going process. Where it stops will be decided not by this House but by the people of Scotland." Scottish nationalism is not a transitory phenomenon. It is unlikely that the Labour and Conservative parties will regain their pre-SNP status. The basic force for Scottish nationalism and devolution is essentially popular, not elitist. If one looks at the various polls, it is clear that at least 60% of the Scots want some form of governmental change that is at least as drastic as that recently proposed by the Callaghan government. Support for independence is roughly at 20%.

Thus, although the SNP is for independence, the polls continue to show that some sort of autonomy short of independence is preferred by a majority of Scots. The nationalism of the majority is a nationalism within the United Kingdom, giving Scottish politics a national dimension whose constituional structure remains to be resolved.

Scotland may well be the prototype of a new type of limited ethnic-nationalism, radical yet non-violent, and demand only the proper amount of control over its economic and political destiny. Thus the process of trans-national integration in Europe occurs simultaneously with regional disintegration.

The injection of this sub-state system into trans-national policies will affect not only the substance of these policies but also the method of bargaining. Scotland will inevitably exert influence on British and European policy making. Indeed, in 1975 there was established the Bureau of

Unrepresented Nationalities in Brussels, one channel through which sub-state systems such as Scotland can seek assistance from the European Community. The politicization and institutionalization of ethnic cleavages in Western Europe results in a tri-level interaction. (12) Scotland is likely to remain a political component of the Europe of tomorrow significantly affecting trans-national policies in Europe.

NOTES

(1) E.g. Richard Rose, Politics in England, 2nd ed. (Boston: Little, Brown, 1974).

(2) The best analysis of the social, class, and ethnic basis of the SNP is by Jack Brand, "The Development of National Feeling in Scotland, 1945-1977" an unpublished paper delivered at the 1977 annual meeting of the American Political Science Association in Washington. Brand concludes his paper:

> In the long run the argument of this paper is that the success of the National party over the last decade is to be explained by the fact that it has come to be regarded by a larger and larger proportion of the Scottish electorate as 'the Party for Scotland.' Not unreasonably, the needs of Scotland are perceived as being very great and an organisation which put this case vigorously and was not associated with the lack of success which had dogged the older parties, was in a very strong position. The details of its stand on the constitutional issue for the majority of its recruits simply was not important. The important factor was that peoples' living standards were low in their own eyes and the new mechanism was sought to improve them. The consciousness of Scottish distinctiveness and the need for expression of the resentment against remote government from London were the essential ingredients in the build up of the new party.

(3) A recent study of Scottish adolescents' views of "My Country" indicates that despite feelings of very low political effectiveness most of the students retained a strong component of "modified Britishness." However all adolescents were exposed to convinced and articulate nationalists among their classmates. See Janet Hartigan, Lafayette College, Pa., unpublished paper delivered at the 1977 Northeastern Political Science Assn. meetings at Mt. Pocono, Pa.

(4) See also "Scottish Nationalism and British Response" in Milton J. Esman (Ed.) Ethnic Conflict in the Western World, (Ithaca, N.Y.: Cornell University Press, 1977). Esman is considered to be the leading specialist on Scottish nationalism in the United States and has written a number of unpublished papers dealing with the SNP.

(5) See Ronald Inglehart, "The Silent Revolution in Europe: Inter Generational Change in Post-industrial Societies," American Political Science Review, December 1971, pp. 991-1017, cited in the chapter by Arend Lijphart "Political Theories and the Explanation of Ethnic Conflict in the Western World" p. 62-3 in Milton J. Esman, op. cit.

(6) "Both the sense of alienation and the concomitant identity crisis is most vehement among the young today. Youth itself, which is a matter of social definition, is simultaneously the locale of the most acute experience of self-estrangement and of the most intensive quest for reliable identities." P. Berger, B. Berger, and H. Kellner, The Homeless Mind: Modernization and Community (New York: Random House, 1974), p. 94, as quoted in W.R. Beer, "Language and Ethnicity in France" Plural Societies, Vol. 7, No. 2 (Summer 1976). Most nationalist movements use "Salami tactics." Most nationalist parties, like the SNP, have no clear ideological focus and receive their finances from a broad spectrum of small and medium-size enterprises. The only firm supporting the SNP that is known abroad is Bell's whiskey distillers, one of the smaller distilleries.

(7) At this time also, Labour M.P. and political science professor John Mackintosh published his influential argument for home rule in his The Devolution of Power, Local Democracy, Regionalism, and Nationalism (London: Charles Knight, 1968).

(8) Democracy and Devolution: Proposals for Scotland and Wales, CMND. 5732. For an excellent account of devolution see James Kellas and Raymond Owen, Devolution and the Political Context in Scotland, unpublished paper delivered at the American Political Science Assn. 1977 meeting in Washington.

(9) Our Changing Democracy: Devolution to Scotland and Wales, CMND. 6348. This White Paper was still rather general and ambiguous, especially the sections on the Scottish Assembly's powers. The key provisions are:

169. These proposals will create for Scotland an elected Assembly which across a great range of subjects will take over the work of Parliament; and they will create a Scottish Executive which, in these subjects, will have wide responsibilities now borne by the Government.

170. There are some specific restrictons and some general constitutional safeguards, but in practice formal intervention by the Government should be exceptional. Within the devolved fields - notably local government, extensive law functions, health, social work, education, housing, physical planning, the environment, roads and traffic, crofting, most aspects of forestry and many aspects of transport - the Scottish Assembly will pass laws and the Scottish Executive will control administration. Organization and policies in these fields will be a matter for them. To finance what they want to do they will have a block grant from United Kingdom taxation which they can allocate as they wish. They will be able, if they choose, to levy a surcharge on local government revenue.

171. Scottish Ministers - the Secretary of State for Scotland the Lord Advocate - will continue to have a major role, as Part V explains. In broad terms however control of the great bulk of public services which affect the people of Scotland will be in the hands of the new Scottish institutions.

(10)   Devolution to Scotland and Wales: Supplementary Statement, CMND. 6585.

(11) "Based on the likely international boundary in the North Sea between Scotland and England at least 70% of the oil reserves would go to an independent Scotland (though this would be considerably less if Shetland went with England rather than Scotland)." Brian W. Hogwood and B. Guy Peters, "Politics and the Economics of Scottish Natonalism," paper delivered before the Social Science History Association, Ann Arbor, Michigan, October 21-23, 1977, p. 22.

(12) For an excellent discussion see Joseph R. Rudolph, Jr., "Ethnic Sub-States and the Emergent Politics of Tri-Level Interaction in Western Europe," The Western Political Quarterly, Vol. XXX, No. 4, December 1977, pp. 537-557.

11 Ethno-Regional Movements, International Alliances, and NATO
Guy Heraud

Among the various aspects of domestic political life which affect international relations and, in particular, the functioning of alliances are the ethno-regional movements which are currently taking shape throughout the entire world. This chapter seeks to analyze the impact of this development and explore means of remedying whatever harmful effects it may have. The chapter will be organized around four themes:

1. The typology of ethno-regional movements,
2. Their impact on alliances,
3. A search for solutions,
4. The case of NATO.

TYPOLOGY OF ETHNO-REGIONAL MOVEMENTS

One should begin by distinguishing between sub-national regionalism and ethnic nationalism. In the first case, that of sub-national regionalism, centrifugal aspirations accept the national framework and aim only at the recognition, the upholding, or the increase of autonomy.   The Bavarian movement in Germany, the Sicilian movement in Italy, the Normand movement in France, and the Asturian movement in Spain all fall into this category, since the adherence of the regions in question to these respective states is not contested. These regionalists belong to the nations which these states represent: they do not present themselves as the people of a distinct nation. In the second case, that of ethnic nationalism, centrifugal aspirations are in conflict with the state itself: they articulate a nationalism which is distinct from the nationalism expressed by the state and seek to constitute a separate state or to join another state already in existence. In every case, this is indicative of a separatist will. The abortive revolt of the Ibos in Nigeria, the partly successful action of the blacks of southern Sudan, the rebellion of the Moros in the Philippines, the creation of Bangladesh, the platform of the Parti Québécois, (1) and the avowed goals of the Basque ETA are all examples of ethnic nationalism. Instead of calling for a simple change within the state, these movements fight (or fought) against the state itself, which they consider foreign, illegitimate, and oppressive. It is thus the presence or the absence of a separatist will which permits one to draw a distinction between simple sub-national regionalism and ethnic nationalism.

It is comparatively easy to distinguish between these two phenomena in the abstract; it is more difficult to deal with their qualifications in the concrete. The distinction between sub-national regionalism and ethnic nationalism is easily applied on the level of avowed intentions: the Parti Québécois, for example, declares itself "independentist," and the Basque ETA is wedded to the idea of creating an "independent and socialist Basque state." The distinction is more unwieldy, however, when considered on the level of hidden intentions. Certain autonomist movements conceal separatist movements; whereas others are sincere. Only through examining the behavior of these movements can one discover their real attitudes. One outward sign, however, may be helpful. When the movement in question is outbidded by another more radical movement, the former is presumably of a purely autonomist rather than separatist nature. The birth of a Corsican Liberation Front, for example, confirms the purely autonomist character of the Union of the Corsican People of the Simeoni brothers, which is indeed the goal always claimed by the Union.

Another difficulty arises when one tries to assess the attitudes of an entire population. Opinion polls, election results, and referenda, if they are held, permit one to get an idea of public sentiment. It must never be forgotten, however, that the latter are essentially evolutive; rather than expressing the profound aspirations of a people, they represent what the population considers feasible at a given moment in history. In this sense it can be said that the elites involved represent the will of the people better than universal suffrage. (2) A number of autonomist movements are the expression of separatist aspirations which are temporarily unattainable; thus, the electoral results achieved by autonomous movements minimize the real importance of separatist currents and conceal their future chances of success.

Finally, the distinction between regionalism and ethnic nationalism does not lie in a present difference in attitudes, but in a difference in objectives; this is a function of the nature of the collectivity. Ethnic nationalism, latent or expressed, exists whenever the collectivity possesses distinctive cultural characteristics within the states; most often these characteristics are associated with the existence of a separate language. (3) On the other hand, whenever a collectivity which is disturbed by centrifugal tendencies lacks a distinct culture - when it has no separate language - one can almost always be assured that regionalist tendencies are involved.

These propositions demand a discussion which would be out of place here. Let it suffice to relegate this subject to sociolinguistic and ethno-political inquiry or, more simply, to patent observation. Ethnic nationalism, also referred to as national liberation movement, appears in the Western world only in those regions which have a language different from the state: the

Basque country, Brittany, Catalonia, Scotland, the Faeroe Islands, Friesland, Wales, Kossovo, the Slovenes of Carinthia and Italy, South Tyrol, the Valley of Aosta, the Ukraine, Georgia, the Baltic States, and Quebec, to name a few. Even if the language is not spoken throughout the entire territory or, where it has survived, is not spoken by all the native inhabitants, it serves as a national cultural symbol. This may be observed in Scotland and, more clearly, in Brittany and the Basque country. At first glance, the problem of the Catholics in Northern Ireland appears to be somewhat different since this population has lost the use of Gaelic. (4) Some observers only see a simple social question there, an obvious error since social alienation is the product of ethnic cleavage. This cleavage seems to be of a religious nature at first, but, upon looking more closely, one realizes that the Catholics are descendants of the Irish autochthons who spoke Gaelic, while the Protestants descended from English and Scottish settlers.

The antagonism which exists between Serbs and Croats is more difficult to explain, since Croatian only differs slightly from Serbian. (5) It must thus be ascribed to a duality of cultures in which religion and history are the key factors. It should be observed that the region is situated on the route from the Orient and that, outside the Western world, religion still plays an important role in national life. Because of this, religious factors are sometimes more important than linguistic ones. The India-Pakistan duality has a religious base rather than a linguistic one, although Hindi and Urdu are closely related to one another. The Moslems demanded their own state in order to escape domination by the Hindus. In a similar fashion, the revolt of the Moros in the Philippines reflected the Moslem opposition to Christian authority. In the Lebanese conflict one Arab-speaking community opposes another. In Ceylon there is tension between the Hindu Cinghalais and the Buddhist Tamouls. It is also evident that religion plays as important a role as language in the Greek-Turkish conflict in Cyprus.

Racial factors should also be mentioned since these also appear to play a predominant role. The Mutu-Tutsi conflict which tears Burundi apart periodically, and the centrifugal movements in southern Sudan and South Mauritania are but two examples. In the United States the question of the blacks has been handled as a national problem. Whenever a separate language - or the culture it expresses - is lacking separatist tendencies are inexistent.

THE IMPACT OF ALLIANCE

Centrifugal movements have an impact on the state in three ways. They weaken the state in which they occur. They generate a risk of inter-state conflict. They also carry the risk of outside intervention.

The Weakening of the State

Centrifugal movements weaken the state as much on a moral level as on a material level, causing harmful effects on internal as well as international order.

Within the state, cohesion may be weakened so much that it incites "non-civic" actions. The Sudeten unrest in 1938, however justified it may have been, is an example of this.

Outside the state, its prestige is compromised. The dissatisfaction of minorities and discontent within its borders are evidence against the democratic and social character of its institutions. The existence of centrifugal forces proves either that the state is not a true nation or that it has been unable to give its diverse populations the advantages which they have expected of it. A concern for reputation abroad leads all states to deny centrifugal demands, or to term them unjust. In the Soviet Union, and even in Yugoslavia, for example, the term "nationalism," taken in its pejorative sense, is used to accuse those who make nationalist demands of impropriety and crime. This is a strange reversal when one thinks of the favor with which socialist countries regard nationalist movements in the Third World. Sometimes a state, recognizing the existence of centrifugal demands, attributes them to purely economic causes; such is the tendency in France where minority problems are stripped of linguistic or cultural significance. Thus it is claimed that Brittany, Occitania, and even Corsica suffer from insufficient economic development, but not from linguistic and cultural alienation.

Centrifugal movements also contribute to the weakening of the state on the material level, especially when they take a quasi-insurrectional course. One may observe this in Spain, where the armed struggle of the Basque ETA is now raging, as well as in Algeria, where for seven years pacification consumed considerable resources and led to the mobilization of a significant military and police effort.

The state is also weakened by the corruption which repression inevitably generates. The danger which the OAS represented to French democracy, for example, was the direct result of the war in Algeria. The Catholic and Protestant organizations of Northern Ireland also pose a threat which may have an impact beyond their own borders.

The Risk of Inter-State Conflict

The inter-state conflict caused by centrifugal movements may take one of two forms: it may appear as a conflict between allies or a conflict with a neutral power of another bloc. In the first case, the alliance is threatened directly. The Cypriot affair is an example of this, since the dispute between Greece and Turkey has put NATO in a tenuous position. Turkey is in a particularly strong position because it is such an important NATO ally, a fact which permits it to hold out the threat of diminished cooperation, if not total withdrawal into neutralism. The Bangladesh conflict has gotten the Western world into difficulties as well, since Pakistan considers any expression of approval of secession a hostile gesture and moves toward neutralism accordingly.

The Risk of Outside Intervention

In certain respects Bangladesh represents a simple case of exacerbated regionalism since the Moslem Bangladesh does not oppose the Islamic principle on which Pakistan is founded. However, it also illustrates the point that national conflicts or exacerbated regionalism can provoke foreign intervention - by India in this case - and thus challenge the alliance. The alliance must intervene and run the risk of war, or yield and suffer the loss of prestige and substance. How Hitler used the German minorities in Europe to weaken, even to destroy, the states which opposed his hegemony is well remembered.

Foreign intervention need not necessarily be military in nature. It may also take the form of economic intervention or commercial embargo. Such actions do not, however, constitute any lesser threat to world peace. The mildest form of outside intervention comes from officially neutral international organizations, such as the United Nations. In actuality, whatever services it may render, mediation by the United Nations is rarely neutral and conceals a power shift in the relations between blocs.

The weakening of individual states, the risk of inter-state conflict, the risk of foreign intervention, and the crises provoked by centrifugal forces in one of its members always weaken or discredit the alliance. Furthermore, national liberation movements carry the risk of revolutionary upheaval with uncontrollable effects. Not only is social order in the various states jeopardized through a chain reaction, the maintenance of the alliance itself is put in question. These are the reasons why every alliance must take precautions to prevent the development of explosive situations within its member states, especially when these are due to ethnic nationalism.

THE SEARCH FOR SOLUTIONS

From this perspective, the distinction between regionalism and national liberation movements takes on special significance. Actually, the first can be appeased with a simple retailoring of the state's territorial structures, whereas the second will only be satisfied by modification of the state's borders. Every solution which falls short of this will be considered insufficient. The customary revolutionary aspirations of national liberation movements reinforce their separatist demands to a considerable degree.

Nevertheless, these two situations have some points in common. To what extent, for example, does the alliance have an interest in interfering in the domestic affairs of its members? Is it in its interest to exercise sufficient force to compel them to evolve in the desirable direction? The conflicts in Cyprus and the Middle East illustrate that NATO, the United States, and the Soviet Union have the utmost difficulty in persuading the parties involved to make the sacrifices necessary in order to bring about a lasting solution to these disputes. The development of a parliamentary assembly similar to the Council of Europe, the Western European Union, or NATO might encourage the search for solutions and increase the chances of seeing them accepted. A certain international consensus tends to develop within these institutions, and the double role - international and national - of the parliamentarians may help ensure that a decision taken by the alliance is ratified by the parliaments and governments of the individual member states. The authority exercised by the alliances and their parliamentary assemblies should not, however, be overestimated; until a true supra-national sovereignty is established, the deputies who compose these assemblies will remain national deputies above all.

The alliance's task is easier when it only has to guarantee a solution previously adopted within the domestic order or one which the state favors. Finland, for example, had no difficulty accepting the decision of the Council of the League of Nations in 1920 concerning the autonomy and Swedish identity of the Aaland Islands. Finding a solution is still easier when a reciprocal situation exists between two countries, such as in the agreements reached between Denmark and Germany concerning the cultural rights of the Danish minority in southern Schleswig and the German minority in northern Schleswig. (6) If one now examines not only the form but also the content of these solutions, it is apparent that national liberation movements raise the important question of the right of self-determination. Although endorsed at innumerable international conventions and inscribed in the political philosophy of most democracies (the Revolution of 1789, the Italian Risorgimento, the October Revolution), the right of self-determination is often denied. (7) Only in the relations between metropole and colony has it received generalized applications. (8) Therein lies one of the greatest contradictions between principle and practice. It is certain that such hypocrisy does not facilitate establishing cordial relations among peoples, but provokes bitterness, resentment, and legitimate revolt. It is thus advisable to grant the right of self-determination to those who have a right to it and wish to make use of it. (9)

There is, however, an obstacle to doing this: the sovereignty of states. In the name of its prestige and national interest, the state almost always opposes the exercise of the right of self-determination through the judicial and coercive means which guarantee its sovereignty. Ceding territory, even if the constitution provides for the possibility, always appears to be an intolerable solution for the state. (10) It must be recognized that the current inter-state order, rife with rivalries and threats of war, is not conducive to states freely accepting territorial modifications which threaten to weaken them appreciably and alter the international balance of power.

In order to institutionalize the right of self-determination, states will have to federate at the same time. The first step, however, will be the most difficult, since the history of federations shows that every federated nucleus exerts an irresistible attraction on its surrounding territories.

Although federalism can be regarded as the condition of generalized self-determination, it also lessens the drawbacks associated with this; successions of governmental leaders take place within the same political entity rather than outside it, and, therefore, they do not threaten the equilibrium between two rival entities. Through federalism, border changes become simple shifts in boundaries. De-dramatized, separatism disappears.

On the other hand, federalism imposes unity where it might be feared that quenching centrifugal tendencies would cause excessive fragmentation. Federalism expresses and harmonizes not only the unity which our societies require, but also the diversity which the respect for multiple identities implies. Moreover, federalism, as a global doctrine (11) bears an economic and social message based on autonomy and broad participation, which is consistent with channeling the revolutionary impulse of the national liberation movements in a peaceful and genuinely democratic direction.

THE CASE OF NATO

Let us see how these ideas may be applied to the North Atlantic Treaty Organization.

Of the 15 members of NATO, only Iceland, Luxembourg, Norway, and Portugal offer perfect ethnic homogeneity, and this is accompanied by linguistic plurality in Luxembourg and Norway. In Luxembourg, French, German, and the Luxembourg dialect are spoken; in Norway there is competition between Bokmål (Dano-Norwegian) and Nynorsk (neo-Norwegian). In both countries, however, the whole population is interested in the usage of the idioms of the other language(s). In the Grand Duchy, the different linguistic groups are not distributed on a geographical basis, and in Norway this distribution takes place according to a city-country cleavage. (12) As a result, neither state has been exposed to ethnic antagonism. Paradoxically, Portugal, which is practically as linguistically homogeneous as Iceland, has experienced a degree of separatism in the Azores and in Madeira. Essentially motivated by the fear that a Communist government would be installed in Lisbon, these separatist tendencies seem to have been allayed by the consolidation of Portuguese democracy.

If the remaining 11 members possess ethnic minorities, they are far from creating problems. Sometimes these are small minorities which have been granted satisfactory status; such is the case of the Frisians (15,000), the Danes of southern Schleswig (50,000), the Germans of northern Schleswig (23,000), the Faroeians (37,000), and the Eskimos, or "Greenlanders," of Denmark. The reciprocity of the minority situation in Germany and Denmark has facilitated making an arrangement which is advantageous for both minorities and thus has established cordial relations between the two allies. Considerably more important is the minority of 420,000 Frisian-speaking people concentrated in the Netherlands Province of Friesland. Although little is mentioned of them, this group has obtained important linguistic rights in the schools, in the administration, and in the mass media; they enjoy considerable autonomy at the communal level.

France is a special case. The European portion of its territory encompasses seven allogeneous ethnic groups whose languages survive in one way or another. However, a long-term policy of cultural assimilation combined with the unifying effect of the Revolution and subsequent wars, especially World War I, has long since silenced them. Their current revival is still embryonic, even in Corsica. Neither domestic order nor the conditions under which France participates in NATO are currently affected by the development of ethno-regionalist movements.

This is also the case in Italy, which has succeeded, through tact and concessions, in circumventing the south Tyrolian demands for self-determination. By the Treaty of Osimo on November 10, 1975, Rome and Belgrade settled the problem of Trieste and finalized the measures dealing with the ethnic minorities on both sides of the border on a reciprocal basis. Only the Slovenes in the province of Udine who, unlike those in Gorizia and Trieste, have been Italians since 1866 do not benefit from any special linguistic rights. As for the Valley of Aosta, the degree of autonomy which has been granted and the indifference of France regarding the Aosta Valley issue explains why this region has never caused any difficulties. The people of Sardinia, Friuli, Occitania, and Piedmont as well as other Gallo-Italians, are in the same situation of tentative reawakening as the allogeneous ethnic groups in France.

In the last decade the United States has demonstrated a new interest in the languages spoken by the numerous ethnic groups dispersed throughout its vast territory. (13) In general, immigrants accept, even desire, integration and assimilation into their new homeland. The question of the blacks appears to be in the process of being solved, and the number of extremists, such as the members of "Black Panthers" has declined since the 1960s. However, Puerto Ricans, Panamanians and American Indians could bring problems of ethnic nationalism to the United States. Yet the Indian question, despite the international attention it has begun to attract (14) does not appear as if it will threaten domestic order within the United States or NATO. The Canal Zone and Puerto Rico, on the other hand, could give rise to dangerous developments due to Spanish-American and Third World solidarity and to the proximity of Cuba. However, the first problem appears to be on the way to resolution and the second is not very pronounced, since at the present time the majority of Puerto Ricans continue to favor Commonwealth status. (15)

In terms of this survey, serious problems of sub-state nationalism affect only five members of NATO: Belgium, Canada, the United Kingdom, Greece, and Turkey. Some of these situations do not appear to have external consequences. The question of ethnic and regional structures in Belgium, for example, is in the process of being resolved. (16) The "devolution" laws currently under preparation will defuse the Welsh and Scottish nationalist movements. Two other situations, however, have obvious international ramifications: the Cyprus dispute between Greece and Turkey, both members of the Alliance, and the question of Northern Ireland, which involves the United Kingdom, a member of the Alliance, and the neutral state of Ireland. In the Irish question, the domestic situation affects the international situation, whereas the reverse is true in the Cyprus affair. Finally, there remains Quebec, an important case which is difficult to classify. No doubt it is primarily a domestic Canadian affair, although Paris has followed the situation with interest ever since 1967 when de Gaulle gave a speech at City Hall in Montreal on the promotion of the rights of the Québécois people. (17) More recently the Quebec Prime Minister's visit to Paris (October-November 1977) revived tensions between Paris and Ottawa.

Each of these problems may be solved temporarily according to the usual methods of domestic politics and diplomacy, but in order to achieve a lasting settlement, it will be necessary to resort to federalism and self-determination. The first step would be to encourage a federal union among the nine members of the European Community. A European Federation would present a double advantage. On the one hand it would restore a balance to NATO which is currently overpowered by the United States; on the other hand, its diffusion over all of Europe would encourage other states to join, unleashing a liberal evolution. The moral and political authority of the Federation of the nine would be sufficiently great to serve as the inspiration for a new type of society, neither collectivist nor capitalist, a society completely federalist in accordance with the socio-economic philosophy of Proudhon and Alexandre Marc. Within this Federation of the Nine, the Irish problem would find a comfortable solution, such as a combination of reunification with Ireland and federalism, with Connaught, Leinster, Munster, and Ulster autonomous. The Protestants of Northern Ireland could accept a solution of this kind because returning Belfast to Ireland within the framework of a federated Europe would no longer mean completely severing their judicial and political ties with the United Kingdom.

The Federation of the Nine would also facilitate the peaceful evolution of the Scottish, Welsh, Flemish and Walloon autonomous movements, as well as those which are maturing in France and Italy. Self-determination of ethnic and regional groups could be organized to allow each to obtain its desired status without this resulting in the weakening of the whole. Regions which currently extend beyond the borders of a single state would have the liberty to define and organize themselves as they saw fit. (18)

There still remains the case of the states outside the Federation. For some of them - Spain, Greece, Portugal, Iceland, Norway - admission would come in the normal course of things. The accession of Turkey (demographically and sociologically a non-European power) on the other hand, would hardly seem advisable; it is not without reason that it does not figure among the candidates for admission to the European Community. The United States, for its part, would neither want nor be permitted to join a federation which it would completely imbalance. Moreover, the presence of the United States would prevent any search for a third economic and social path, which is both the desire and the interest of the European nations. Canada, finally, could not envision joining a political organization to which the United States did not belong.

It follows from these observations that NATO plus Ireland could constitute a double network of concentric interdependencies: the European Federation (a political, economic and military body), North America, and Turkey. Within the whole, connected in this way, unresolved questions could be dealt with more easily. As for Cyprus, presumably the creation of a federation would revive the conditions of the dispute and facilitate formulating a system of guarantees. In Quebec this would make possible a "sovereignty-association" type of solution, which seems inevitable in the long run. A European Federation would also offer an economic and cultural counterweight for the six million people of Quebec who are currently lost in the mass of 240 million Anglo-Saxon North Americans.

NOTES

(1) cf Pierre Maugué, La victoire du Parti québécois, in L'Europe en Formation, no. 204, March 1977.

(2) An historic example of this is the contrast between de Gaulle's appeal of June 18, 1940 and the strong majority of parliamentarians voting in favor of July 10 devolution laws who rallied in Vichy. Who represented the interests and the profound desires of France? The country's representatives or the rebel general? What is valid for the French is also valid for other ethnic groups. Poor electoral results should not necessarily discredit other autonomous groups. As a specialist on the subject writes, "the spokesman of an ethnic or linguistic group can only be one who will fight for the existence of his people, the defense of his language and the survival and prosperity of the ethnicity group to which he belongs." Theodor Veiter, Le droit de libre disposition du peuple jurassien expertise fondée sur le droit international public, Vienne-Stuttgart, W. Braumuller, 1971, p. 155.

(3) cf Francois Fontan, Ethnisme, Bagnols-sur-Cèze, 1975; Sergio Salvi Le Nazioni proibite, Valecchi, Florence, 1973; Meic Stephens, Linguistic Minorities in Western Europe, Gomer Press, Llandysul Dyfels, 1976.

(4) cf Guiu Sobiela-Caanitz, "L'Irlande du Nord" in Contre les Etats, les regions d'Europe, Paris-Nice: Presses d'Europe, 1973.

(5) For the opposite opinion see: Branko Franolic, La langue littéraire croate, Colloquia parisiensia I, Paris: Nouvelles Editions Latines, 1972.

(6) cf my article: "Le Sleswig, région frontalière modèle," in Contre les Etats, op. cit. pp. 162-174.

(7) cf my study: "Le droit d'autodétermination des peuples entre l'hypocrisie et l'accomplissement" in Le féderalisme et Alexandre Marc, Lausanne: Centre de Recherches européenes, 1974, pp. 125-145.

(8) According to the artificial and comic "salt water theory."

(9) Among the numerous aspects of the whole problem of self-determination are: 1) the question of which territories have access to it 2) the question of its repetition. As far as the first point is concerned, one should distinguish between "minorities by dint of circumstance" (Minorities in diaspora and in enclaves) for which a territorial demarcation is impossible or leads to the creation of entities which are too small or are mixed up within the territories belonging to another ethnic group; and "minorities through men's mistakes", that is to say minorities which are adjacent to a homoethnic State from which they have been arbitarily separated by a bad treaty.

(a) For the "minorities by dint of circumstance, " the right to decide their own fates cannot go so far as succession. They will have to satisfy themselves with territorial autonomy, if a sufficiently important territory exists which can be delimited, or simply with cultural autonomy (cf Theodor Veiter, Die nationale Autonomie, Vienna, 1938).

(b) The right of self-determination, on the other hand, will have to be fully recognized, as nothing stands in the way of "minorities through men's mistakes." The thesis that only "whole peoples," should benefit from this right should be vigorously opposed. No moral, logical or legal reason justifies this limitation; it is simply a reflection of political opportunism.

It must be possible to hold referenda on self-determination at the request of the people. Ethnic feeling awakens gradually, and it would be unfair to arrest it before it is fully expressed. On these points, see my work, L'Europe des ethnies, Paris-Nice Presses d'Europe, 1974, p. 169-270. On the entire problem: Heinz Kloss, Grundfragen der Ethnopolitik, Vienne-Stuttgart: Breumüller, 1969. Adde: Kurt Rabl, Das Selbstbestimmungsrecht der Völker, Munich, 1963.

(10) cf Luc Saidj, La notion de territoire en droit public francais contemporain, doctoral thesis in law at the University of Lyon, III. 1972.

(11) Federalism as a global doctrine is often inappropriately referred to as "integral federalism." It comes from Proudhon, and its greatest proponent is the philosopher, Alexandre Marc. In contrast to all the "monisms," including liberalism and marxism, federalism is an open doctrine, a methodology based on the most modern scientific techniques. This is the only organized thinking on pluralism, autonomy, participation and cooperation which exists. Cf Alexandre Marc, La dialectique du déchainement and De la méthodologie a la dialectique, Paris-Nice; Presses d'Europe, Adde: Reperes pour un fédéralisme révolutionaire, a special number of the periodical, L'Europe en Formation 190-192, January-March 1976; Karl Hahn, Föderalismu, die demokratische Alternative, Munich: E. Vogel, 1975; Lutz Rocemheld, Integraler Föderalismus, Modell für Europa, 2 volumes, Munich: E. Vogel 1977.

(12) cf Harald Haarmann, Soziologie und Politik der Sprachen in Europa, Munich: DTV, Wissenschaftliche Reihe, 1975, pp. 333-336.

(13) Under the influence, among others, of Joshua A. Fishman, cf Heinz Kloss, Das Nationalitätenrecht der Vereinigten Staaten von Amerika, Vienna-Stuttgart: W. Braumuller, 1963.

(14) of which the international meeting in Geneva during the summer of 1977 is the proof.

(15) Heinz Kloss, op. cit., pp. 242-252.

(16) cf my study "La Belgigue en marche vers le fédéralisme," L'Europe en Formation, periodical cited, no. 209-210, August-September 1977.

(17) The attitude of the French government is concisely expressed in the statement of Prime Minister Raymond Barre (Le Monde, November 8, 1977): "France has a policy of non-interference in the affairs of Canada, especially in the internal affairs of Quebec ... We think that it is for the Québécois to determine their own future. We are not indifferent about that future, because Quebec is the most important French-speaking industrialized community in the world outside of France, and because we have a number of other reasons to be interested in what takes place in Quebec. We cannot therefore be indifferent about the destiny of the Québecois, and we are ready to help them, whatever road they choose. But it is not for us to determine that road."

(18) cf Fried Esterbaurer, Formen und Methoden transnationaler Raumplanung europäischer Grenzregionen, Publications of the Austrian section of the CIFE, no. 3, Vienne-Stuttgart: W. Braumüller, 1977.

12 Theory or Illusion? The New Nationalism As a System Concept
Walter Goldstein

The crisis consists precisely in the fact that the old order is dying and the new cannot be born; in this interregnum a great variety of morbid symptoms appears.

Gramsci, Prison Notebooks

The purpose of this symposium is to test the validity of a theoretical innovation in the literature of international relations. The preceding papers in this volume examined the empirical referents and the structural components of the New Nationalism. It must now be determined whether these pieces of theory can be put together in a useful manner. It must also be asked whether this exercise in integration is a creative endeavor or just the latest fad to enter the literature of political science.

Any exercise in theory must begin with a definition of terminology and particular attention must be paid in this case to the usages of system analysis. Most theorizing about the New Nationalism implies, explicitly or not, that a form of system dominance distinguishes the contemporary world order. It is assumed that systemic forces have come to regulate the conduct of international commerce; and that the behavior of 150 nation-states has been largely determined by the economic constraints within the international system - in short, that national regimes have been forced to adjust their domestic politics to the external pressures that operate, somewhat autonomously and largely beyond their control, in the world order. The New Nationalism therefore explains, with theoretical flourishes added, why national regimes resort to chauvinist and isolationist rhetoric as their economic livelihood becomes more and more constricted by the competitive rigor in the world trade system. (1)

Most theorists in the past asserted that nation-states will normally adjust their domestic strategy to the interplay of external pressures, but it must now be asked whether states do in fact succeed in adapting to external change. In many cases it is obvious that national actors have failed; their domestic politics remained immobile as the threat of economic warfare and global recession intensified. The dislocation prompted by the oil crisis, inflation and monetary instability has been unprecedented. It created a major upheaval in each of the leading economies and it revealed the full extent to which national regimes failed to adjust to externally derived rules. Some were driven to the verge of bankruptcy.

The record shows that some states suffer more severely from the new rules of interdependence than do their neighbors. States conventionally viewed as super-powers are less constrained than middle powers or the less developed countries (LDCs); they enjoy wider policy choices and a larger room for diplomatic maneuver. However in the last resort they, too, must recognize the burden of systemic restrictions. In formulating domestic policy and strategic plans they have become inhibited, though to a lesser extent than their neighbors, in coping with the economic conflicts and the monetary surges that disturb the international order. (2)

A few examples can illustrate the tensions that divide the world into rival hierarchies of national wealth or into regional struggles for economic power. It can be determined at a later point whether an international division of labor - or a class war - has come to dominate world politics.

For a start, tidal sweeps of inflation and hot money have engulfed every nation in the system. Whether it is a "locomotive" or a dependent actor, each nation has had to adjust its currency values, its government deficits, and its balance of payments to better manage its domestic demand curves. Economic recovery schedules have been cut back, largely because international markets contracted and export trade was sharply curtailed. In the scramble to keep up with the increasing price of energy and raw materials, nations resorted to trade war measures to finance their energy imports and to expand their hard currency earnings. Liberal or collectivist regimes, alike, prepared to beggar their neighbors in tariff or trade rivalries. Each sought to promote its industrial productivity at home and to advance its standing in the world hierarchy of economic power. (3)

It now appears that the pressures of economic interdependency and trade rivalry will be neither transitory in span nor limited in scope. The global trading system has changed radically since 1973; the easier conditions that prevailed in the era of industrial expansion (lasting from 1948 to 1973) are not likely to return. In those years, though the real GNP of most nations doubled, the aggregate flow of international trade multiplied by a factor of five. It was in that belle époque of expansion that industrial nations learned to harmonize their economic growth within a managed system of free trade. The thrust of free trade has greatly diminished in the last five years and it may not be revived in this century. It has been replaced by forced restraints of trade, by the manipulation of exchange values, by the subsidizing of exports, and by the extensive curtailment of domestic growth curves. (4)

A simple example can illustrate the shift from growth to scarcity expectations within the system. At present rates of global recession, only 24,000 giant tankers pass each year (about one every ten minutes) through the narrow exit of the Arabian Gulf. Yet if only one were blown up in the Straits of Hormuz, either by accident or by guerrilla action, the United States would be denied 40% of its energy imports while Europe and Japan would lose more than double that amount. Were the Straits to be blocked for a year, OPEC's export volume would fall by 65% and the price of crude oil would possibly soar from $13 to $50 a barrel. The only nations that could afford such an exorbitant price would be the few that compete aggressively in the world's markets. No matter whether the rest were to resort to deflation, to controls or to rationing at home, they could not hope to alleviate their plight. As the poorest of the LDC's have found, the world trade system deals ruthlessly with nations which depend on neighbors to help sustain their wealth.

Two criticisms should be noted at this stage. Arguing from different premises, critics insist that there is nothing new in the New Nationalism that has not been said before about rational strategy. It is argued that the economic inhibitions of today are not greatly different from the strategic constraints seen in the 1950s and 1960s, when power was polarized between two hostile nuclear camps. No nation could step out of line in those tense days of the Cold War without endangering its bargaining ability within its own alliance or the nuclear protection afforded by its allies. This first criticism is not misplaced but it is exaggerated. The nuclear stalemate between the super-powers (and their respective alliances) was never as constricting as the economic inhibitions found today. Nor did the nuclear "balance of terror" remain intact for long. As the deployment of nuclear weapons multiplied, their deterrent effect was eroded. New initiatives in political maneuver were dared and risk-taking increased, especially in the wars waged in Southeast Asia and the Middle East. A pattern of stable deterrence materialized but the freedom for political maneuver increased.

The second criticism is somewhat literary. Critics have noted the frequency with which theoretical concepts have changed in the literature of political science. In past years theorists have indulged themselves in distinctions between high and low policy, or between sub-systemic and sub-national fissures among nation-states. Theorists focused attention on regional integration, trans-national linkages, the domestication of international tensions, the emergence of post-industrial or elite-driven societies. Particular attention was paid to "communications overload," or to the "neo-functionalist" interpretation of supra-national institutions. The literature generated many illusions about international power but few of them survived. It is alleged that the New Nationalism is only the latest fad to appear in a fast changing field.

THE REALITIES OF SYSTEM DOMINANCE

It is unwise to predict that a new theory will survive when many before have failed. There is a unique reason, however, to believe that the New Nationalism and its constructs of system dominance are here to stay. Both the resource base and the market forces that activate the world's supply and demand curves have turned down sharply. Marxist theorists, liberal economists, multi-national investment planners and Cabinet ministers now share a gloomy prognosis. (6) They anticipate that critical commodities (such as oil and uranium) will be inordinately expensive and scarce within a few years; and that export earnings and industrial employment possibilities will contract. This will force nation-states to scramble for the few opportunities for expansion that open up; and not even the fortunate nations, such as the oil exporters, can look forward to an untroubled future. Monetary instability has already hit the dollar and other currencies, while the course of inflation has increased unemployment across the world. Living standards and real GNP have begun to decline for the first time in thirty years, and productive investments have dried up in many continents. There are no enclaves left to shelter the wealth of the few or to insulate a nation's economy from the onset of a system-wide depression. (7)

A remarkable development occurred as the pace of economic crisis began to escalate. The political forces of nationalism intensified at the same time that the economic survivability of the nation-state was called into question. Domestic factions came to exercise a growing constituency pressure upon national governments to protect them from the rough turmoil of world trade. This resort to neo-mercantile strategy on the part of political parties and pressure groups was easy to understand but impossible to implement. In practically no case can a government take effective action on a unilateral basis to withstand, let alone to reverse, the crushing impact of external change. (8)

In most states the capability to stimulate growth and to redistribute material benefits has severely diminished. Welfare spending and public expenditures have had to be cut and the money supply curtailed. There has been a grave overload of demand on the domestic politics of allocating national wealth. In clamoring for a larger piece of the national income, especially as inflation escalates, millions of voters have behaved as if the autonomy of the national economy were still intact and as if the resources of the nation could still be husbanded by defensive action. The rising rancor in European or Canadian politics reveals that groups on the left and the right simply do not know how to redistribute a nation's wealth at a time when its wealth base is shrinking and its exports are losing ground.

The worst of contemporary delusions holds that goverent should "do something" to repair a nation's declining fortunes. Political leaders are expected to enlarge the employment, the capital investment, the export surplus and the credit facilities of the nation at a time when recession and inflation have wracked the worldwide system of transactions. It is piously hoped that government will insulate the nation from a worldwide recession, thus protecting its industrial growth plans and its fragile mode of political equilibrium from the rigors of trade war. Some nations have chosen to enlarge the regulatory powers and budgetary authority of the public sector while others have cut back on dirigiste controls to promote the entrepreneurial pursuit of national wealth. Regardless of which method was adopted, the financing of soaring energy import costs has not been met, the force of cost-push inflation has not been blunted, and the outflow of investment funds has not been checked. (9) Historic election struggles were fought in France and Italy but neither succeeded in resolving the urgent problems that each economy has to face.

It is in this context of disrepair that two modes of system integration have failed to work. The first involved such coordinating agencies as GATT and the International Monetary Fund (IMF); the second looked to supra-national organizations, such as the EC and the Andean Pact. In fact, neither of these groups succeeded in rallying the collective agreement or the separate energies of member-states. Rivalries prevailed where joint action might have been productive in harmonizing trade or monetary strategies on a trans-national basis, but corrective action was not taken. The reciprocity rules designed by GATT were disregarded as nations raised tariffs surcharges, non-tariff barriers and orderly marketing arrangements. These classic maneuvers of trade war were matched by a set of monetary manipulations. The fixed exchange rates negotiated at Bretton Woods and the flexible float of the Smithsonian Agreements were abrogated. To steal pecuniary advantages, nations resorted to "dirty floats" and to undermining the "snake in the tunnel" arrangements that were supposed to stabilize currency values. Steel, shipbuilding, textiles, automobiles and electronic appliances were protected by ingenious negotiations, but the cause of multilateral trade negotiation that free traders had once cherished was firmly set aside. (10)

The thrust of the New Nationalism can be gauged in the extent to which nation-states have become reactive rather than initiating actors in today's world order. After the worst years of the Cold War had passed it was believed that economic integration (at least in the West) would replace the negative-sum rivalries and discord that had previously obtained. This belief proved to be naive. As domestic claims for protection increased, governments began to revise the alliance loyalties that had guided their diplomacy. Aggressiveness in economic maneuver was demanded by mass-consumption societies on both sides of the OECD bloc. No longer unified by the ideology of Cold War, political parties and pressure groups called for the staging of statist power plays and mercantilist initiatives to protect their living standards and national accounts.

Nations struggled to keep abreast with their neighbors' devaluations and the trans-atlantic recession by curbing non-oil imports and subsidizing their own exports. Attention switched from the alliance politics of the nuclear super-powers to the financial skirmishing of the three "locomotive" economies (the United States, Japan, and the Federal Republic). The three had previously served as prime movers in directing Multi-Nation Trade Negotiations, (MTN), the North-South Commodity Agreements, the OECD Summit Conferences, and the global energy dialogues. Although their economies were relatively strong, the three began to change their strategy. They either abused their industrial leverage to secure special trading privileges or they took advantage of their monetary position to drive down currency exchange rates. Together with the OPEC bloc, they did little to help the disadvantaged LDCs or to restore stability to the world trade system. It has been argued that hegemonial leadership must be exerted, as Britain showed in the 1890s and the United States tried in the 1950s and 1960s, if the principles of free trade are to be defended. In the 1970s there was no nation that could exert such power, or that could realize the valuable benefits of doing so. Hence, the reversion to economic nationalism and rivalry produced a system that penalized most nations and rewarded none. (11)

THEORY AS A CLASSIFICATION OF BEHAVIOR

An analogy has been drawn between the limited uses of military versus economic power in today's world. The analogy suggests that nations defer to the system if they are forced to do so. When the nuclear era began it was believed that the nation-state had forfeited the "hard wall defensibility" of its territorial boundaries. Theoretically, the military shell of state sovereignty had been smashed; it could no longer guard its citizens against a massive nuclear assault and the demise of the nation-state was widely suspected. The suspicion lost its force as an expectation of stable deterrence replaced the fear of nuclear threat and destruction. Confidence in the rituals of collective diplomacy increased and nations once again pursued divergent security interests. A few cases of military aggression and diplomatic adventurism were attempted but the prevailing nuclear stand-off lasted through the 1960s and 1970s. Minor or middle powers resorted to war as an extension of national policy, as Clausewitz had urged; and it could no longer be argued that the nation-state was "played out" as an independent entity. In short, the state survived the revolutionary consequences that were at first predicted in the development of nuclear weapons. (12)

A second reading of the system domination of national actors was given by theorists who prophesied the forceful, neo-functional integration of nation-states. They predicted that the state would surrender much of its economic sovereignty to the institutional integration (especially in the EC) and the trans-national linkages that had developed in the Western world. They argued that nations would improve their economic performance if they joined regional Common Markets or if they abandoned their financial autonomy to the free movement of finance capital. In a manner reminiscent of Adam Smith, they argued that economic nationalism should be terminated and then an international division of labor should be accepted so that all nations could freely vie to expand their share of world trade. The laws of comparative advantage would therefore limit the role that each economy should pursue in order to specialize in the generating of industrial wealth.

Within a few years these predictions proved to be exaggerated, too. Instead of submitting to the authority of integrating institutions, governments fought them to a standstill. The EC failed to implement the common monetary policy or the regional development rules that the unification planning of the Community required. GATT and the IMF failed to discipline member-states that willfully broke the agreed rules. Entities such as the International Air Transport Association (IATA) the Andean Pact and the International Energy Agency (IEA) began to falter and the North-South negotiations failed to devise a new world order. Functionalist theory explained a limited amount of voluntary and cooperative behavior among nation-states but it underestimated the remainder of their disintegrative activities. (13)

A better classification of the behavior of system-constrained states has been advanced by Wolfram Hanrieder. Most states are to be found securely quartered, as he put it, at the intersection of four systemic forces. (14)

1. Vertically, their domestic economies are yoked by their limited performance in international markets.

2. Horizontally, they are bound together by the struggle to compete with neighbors and trade rivals.

3. Laterally, they are bound into trans-national exchange relations with other actors, such as OPEC, the Bank for International Settlement (BIS), the Euro-dollar banking syndicates, or multi-national oil companies.

4. Supra-nationally, they are confined by the structural rigidities of a hierarchic economic order.

The submission to systemic constraints is by no means complete but it is remarkably pervasive. Some nations have fared well in promoting their national interests within a complex and competitive environment, but most have fallen victim to the interdependence patterns that dominate world trade. A distinction can be drawn between the states that can still fight for their place in the sun and those which cannot. Most of the 24 rich capitalist nations in the OECD bloc have been relatively successful in striking a balance between their domestic needs and their reliance on external resources; a few, such as the United Kingdom, Italy and Portugal, have fared poorly. The command economies among the 12 communist countries and the 115 LDCs have tried to isolate themselves with various statist doctrines and planning instruments but they have not escaped the burdens of their dependent status. The worst hit are those (among the 115 LDCs) which control few productive resources, small export earnings, and currencies too soft to finance trade credits.

The plight of the poor, however, has burdened the systemic order and the fortunes of the rich. Nearly one-third of OECD exports are sold in LDC markets; the profit margins of metropolitan banks depend heavily on loans to weak debtor countries; and the recycling of petro-dollars has moved funds from the Center cities of the old empires to a few of the Periphery capitals of the Third World. (15) Now that they are trapped in a negative-sum game, in which all nations could lose (as happened in the 1930s), the states of the capitalist, the communist, and the Third World bloc have recognized that a system in decline cannot be easily repaired. The course of inflation since 1973 has reduced the prosperity of the affluent, in part by pauperizing more of the poor. That all nations tend to lose when the aggregate level of demand declines is now a salient rule of political economy.

Obviously, individual nations can try to isolate themselves and to ward off systemic constraints. They can print more money, employ their work force in public service jobs, and artificiallyrun down their own exchange values (as the United States has done). However, they cannot stimulate their own export industries, increase their overseas earnings, up-grade their industrial productivity, or expand their capital-intensive economies through unilateral action. To combat a global recession, these benefits, the monetarists argue, can only be realized by retrenching domestic investments and welfare expenditures. Most governments try to avoid such punitive measures, because they suspect that forced retrenchments will be unsuccessful and unpopular, and also unjust. In this regard they face the unenviable choices to be made by New York City, where economic decline is supposed to be countered by cutting welfare services, tax levies, and borrowing limits.

The full weight of these inhibitions can be recognized if an effort is made to subtract the value of services from the GNP recorded by competing nations. The necessity to produce high value-added goods, particuarly for export, then emerges as a critical measure of economic strength. In this calculation it is evident that most industrial nations can finance a high standard of living only if they succeed in earning (as in France or Germany) between 30% and 50% of their remaining GNP from hard-won export incomes. Given a shrinking but competitive world market, this is a difficult target to achieve. At present there is an annual deficit of $45 billion between oil producing and consuming nations, and the credit facilities of the IMF are nearing exhaustion. It is in this context that nations have measured the systemic constraints that determine so many of their policy choices.

ENVIRONMENTAL CHANGES IN WORLD TRADE

Two changes in the environment of international trade have added considerable strength to the dominance of the system. The first appears in the expansion of direct investments and of the multi-national corporations (MNCs) that control them. MNCs are involved in more than 60% of foreign trade transactions; in the United States and many rival economies they account for nearly 60 percent of the value-added to all industrial production. On an aggregate basis, the foreign investments of the leading MNCs are significantly greater than the earnings generated by home-produced export trade. In the case of the United States, for example, several hundred MNCs account for an overseas sales turnover exceeding $400 billion, while conventional exports barely amount to 25% of this sum. The matching figures recorded by the United Kingdom, Holland, Sweden, or Switzerland are no less impressive. (16)

The consequences of these developments can be measured in political terms. The 500 MNCs (and their 49,000 overseas affiliates) surveyed by the United Nations have become eminent decision agents in world trade. Their operations are not immune to the controls exercised by host states, but neither are they particularly helpful to national aspirations. By redeploying their investment funds and production lines from the home country to a cheaper wage economy abroad, they cannot only deplete the jobs and the earnings of domestic industry but they can greatly improve the productivity of foreign competitors. Evidence of such movements can be seen in the relocation of United States electronics, German automobiles, Swiss watches, and Japanese textile industries to the LDCs in Latin America and Southeast Asia. Their assembly plants pay less in weekly wages locally than workers receive in one hour in Detroit, the Ruhr, the Midlands, or the blue-collar cities of Japan. (17)

A second development in the trade environment is related to the first. Enormous movements of Euro-dollars and liquid assets have been initiated by OPEC creditors or multi-national banks. As a result, national accounts have been widely impaired.   Anticipating a devaluation of the lira, the pound sterling, or the French franc, a large number of the MNCs and their international bankers relocated their funds overseas. By securing a higher rate of interest or a better return on their mobile money, the MNCs in many instances helped force the devaluation of their home state's currency. A novel form of dependencia appeared in London, Paris and Montreal as money was shifted through the Euro-dollar market to more promising locations or currencies abroad.

A striking development occurrred when the OPEC leaders moved massive funds out of sterling or when the French banks (many of which were nationalized entities) relocated credit lines from home industry to oil interests in Texas or Brazil. There was little that could be done to match the higher security and the better returns offered overseas. Neither France nor the United Kingdom dared to raise domestic interest rates at a time of extended stagflation. They knew that they could not impair the free flight of investment funds, they could not afford to cut themselves off from world markets by curbing the inflow or the outlfow of MNC credit lines and equity issues. (18)

It has been suggested in the earlier papers of James Caporaso and Edward Morse that a better coordination of national strategy would help to improve the stand-off between competing nation-states. Regrettably, it may be too late to negotiate a better harmony among inter-state transactions. The rules of free trade and voluntary cooperation were followed while most nations shared in rising curve of growth, but most curves have now turned downward. The efforts to coordinate currency fluctuations, to accelerate the MTN discussions in Geneva, to stabilize commodity prices, to reduce Japan's export surplus, or to promote the EEC's monetary consensus have largely failed. A trilateral attempt to regulate reserve currency rates (with Japan and Europe trusting the hegemony of the United States dollar) soon disintegrated. Fearful of domestic inflation, the "locomotive" economies refused to reflate or to increase domestic interest rates. Logically, their allies continued to subsidize key exports (especially in steel and high value-added manufactures) and to discourage import trade.   The MNCs heightened the tension by relocating investments and production plants in countries where political uncertainty and inflation were less pronounced. The only defense measures remaining to most nation-states were not at all productive. They included the resort to selective protectionism, the curbing of domestic demand, the devaluation of currency, and the forced reduction of oil imports.   As expected, these measures intensified the negative-sum loss in total trade and by doing so helped prolong the system-wide recession. (19)

THEORY AND PREDICTION

A realistic depiction of the international system must include one additional element: the structure of international capitalism.   In most regimes the belief is held, though they strenuously deny it, that there is a "natural order" in the maldistribution of welfare equities, growth prospects, and national wealth. One-quarter of the world's population enjoys three-quarters of the stock of wealth; and it is widely believed that this asymmetry reflects the superiority of capitalist enterprise. Western leaders insist that the uneven generation and distribution of wealth is an apt reflection of economic Darwinism. Industry has been more effectively promoted in the West than elsewhere, it is argued; under capitalism, the free use of capital has energized societies to respond to technological change. It is alleged that the collectivist and the non-market economies of the socialist or Third World have failed to match the productive accomplishments of the capitalist states; they have overlooked the human need for a profit motive and they have suppressed the vigorous forces of acquisition that govern a mass-consumption society. On the scales of world history, the inferior standing to which collectivist societies are condemned is supposedly just and immutable.

The contemporary concern with crisis management has revived the political ideology of international capitalism. Whether they are rich, poor, collectivist or unbalanced, most economies honor the capitalist procedures of the world market. Few governments have tried to create alternative sets of rules, and even the most radical of regimes have muted their assaults on the injustices of free trade as a force of imperialism. The revolutionary rhetoric broadcast by Moscow, Peking, Tripoli or the United Nations is beamed largely for domestic consumption. None seriously intend to overthrow, or even disrupt, the punishing bias within the world order.

There may be good reasons for the LDCs to blunt their criticism of Western imperialism. The credits and the advanced technology offered by the rich industrial states are vital to the LDC producers of primary commodities, and they could not be easily replaced. Critics have noted that the terms of trade have moved steadily against the welfare of the poor and in favor of the right in recent years; but they have offered no Grand Design to narrow the income gap or to create a new economic order. As a result, the belief has spread that the triadic division of spoils (between the advanced, the collectivist, and the developing nations) will persist for years to come. Naturally, a few nations will acquire greater wealth (e.g., Singapore or Taiwan) and a few will grow relatively poorer. However, it has become an article of faith, even among the leaders of the command economies, that the trading system will survive as a capitalist structure, presumably with most of its inequities left intact. (20)

The phenomenal interdependence in world trade and investment flows has provoked a second surprise. Nations have not only learned to measure their standing in the conventional usage of the capital market place, they have also come to accept the division of labor that is central to its operation. The evidence on this score is significant. Most nations have come to judge their standing, and each other's, in terms of the capital accumulation and the labor productivity realized in the domestic economy. Nations specializing in capital or technology-intensive industries have gained in superiority in comparison with those whose value-added work is less affluent. The least favored of all are those nations which rely on labor-intensive trade or primary product exports.

Though all states have tried to resist the course of comparative decline, none could afford to ignore the leading shibboleth of the day: the international equalizing of factor costs. If textiles or automobile components can be manufacturered cheaply in MNC plants in Brazil or South Korea, it is argued, there can be no good reason for the failing economies of West Europe (or the East!) to hold on to such unproductive and labor-intensive activities. Attempts to protect or to subsidize marginal manufacturers or textile workers have offended the trans-national managers who resort to conventional theories of economic utility; but neither the workers nor their governments were comforted when trade theorists assured them that alternative sources of income or support could not be secured in a global market experiencing contraction pains.

Adam Smith might have approved of these arguments. He objected to the economic nationalism and the trade protection of the mercantilist era. He urged that states and producers follow the natural division of labor between skilled and cheap labor and the laws of comparative cost. The policy of contemporary governments, whether on the Left or Right, must strongly disagree. They reject the appeal to dismiss whole sectors of the work force or to concede that millions of their citizens are employed in the "wrong" industries. They have firmly insisted that their defense of a high standard of living can not be cut back to a point determined by the international calibrating of labor productivity. Some governments have confessed that the distribution of the national work force, its industrial investments, and its fiscal priorities require serious revision, but few have been strong or willful enough to trim their domestic policies to satisfy the dictates of global market requirements. The United Kingdom and Italy, for example, refused to reduce public expenditure or minimum wage rates even at a time when the IMF required them to contract credit and aggregate demand. However, their refusal was short lived. Britain had to borrow five times from the IMF, and by 1976 its Labour government had been obliged to settle for a highly conservative economic policy.

It is not surprising that governments should try to resist the market dictation of a division of labor. Governments are expected to satisfy the economic illusions and the political compromises that their citizens enact into legislation. In this regard nation-states tend to perform with remarkable consistency. Whether the governing elite is drawn from managers of oligopolies, military juntas, revolutionary idealists, or state capitalists does not matter. There is no way in which nation-states can readily admit that they have been priced out of key markets, or that the next system recession will reduce them to abject poverty. In most cases, governments are obliged to adjust in a temporizing manner before economic realities, but not to confront them with Draconian counter-measures and retrenchment strategies.

Indeed, it is in the conflict between statist illusions and inter-state power plays that the sharpest cutting edge is to be found in the constructs of a New Nationalism. Le roi est mort, vive le roi. Nations everywhere are mortified by their economic insufficiency and by their vulnerability to market change; yet nationalism is alive and the political demands made upon national governments continue to escalate. Though concern for national security and military preparedness remains high, the principal expression of nationalism today is articulated in material anxieties. Clearly, the destiny of the nation-state is neither to submit to a free trade imperium nor to wither away in an international class war. The economic logic of patriotism might grow increasingly absurd, but its political thrust survives. Even if they must live as poor shopkeepers, nations are determined to stay in business.

The New Nationalism suggests, therefore, that the role of the state is to control domestic demands and conflicting claims at a level that corresponds to the nation's standing in the global order. While securing marginal advantages and increments of wealth or employment for the population at home, the managers of the national economy must also cooperate with international efforts to rationalize the world trade system. It is argued also that their cooperation must be forthcoming when their own economy begins to lag in productivity and capital replenishment, since it is the duty of the losers to help protect the continuity of the structure. It is on these grounds that the rich nations have urged the poor to not cancel the repayment of debts and to not increase their tariff barrier defenses.

It is doubtful whether such altruism can be sustained by the fragile political institutions and the shifting coalitions that compose national governments. Whether it does or does not try to regulate or deflate the domestic economy, any government will hesitate to discipline struggling claimants at home so that its comparative standing in the international division of labor can be raised overseas.

Moreover, the external environment of world trade is likely to deteriorate in the next few decades, and this can only complicate the tasks of national planners and management elites. There is already a shortage of oil, of some non-ferrous metals, and of many jobs. It is probable that the shortages will increase during the 1980s and that states will fail to discipline the managers of men or money. The only commodities in surplus will be unskilled labor, both in the rich economies and the LDCs, and there will be a glut of manufacture for which there is an urgent need but insufficient purchasing power. The first skirmishes of trade warfare have already begun and they are likely to escalate in frequency and in intensity as the decade continues. (21)

There are four challenges that nation-states will have to satisfy, simultaneously, if the economic order is to survive. No matter whether it resorts to market strategies or collectivist planning, each government will have to cooperate in the following activities. It will be obliged:

1. to help stabilize the system at a reasonable pace of technical growth and industrial expansion;

2. to help conserve resources in scarce supply and to utilize capacities (both human and material) now lying dormant;

3. to integrate its own growth schedules with those of rival nations, in order to eliminate boom-or-bust spurts, to control trade expansion, the inflation of monetary resources and price surges;

4. to help redistribute the stock of wealth-generating power between Center and Periphery nations, between metropolitan cities and neo-colonial barrios, and between the producers of high and low value-added goods.

A set of reasonable but negative conclusions can be drawn from the proposition that a world of rival states will satisfy practically none of these demands. First, it is evident that a further belle epoque of free trade and harmonious growth is not likely to recur in this century. Second, whether they move independently or in multi-lateral groups, nations will not remove the burden of constraints imposed by a system dominant world, nor will they replace them with alternative structures and procedural rules. In sum, nation-states are too powerfully competitive to collaborate or to wither away. Their interdependent relationships are too pervasive to be easily modified, or overthrown, and they will have to adjust politically to a system that can not easily be budged.

It is this reality that the New Nationalism attempts to gauge. National hostilities and economic interdependence have both grown apace. It is no passing fad of political theorists to conclude that the hierarchy of force in the economic order will dictate the pace of system change. This is sure to occur. What cannot be foreseen is the response capacity of nationalist entities of human society. Will they compete or collaborate? Will they try to resist or submit to the forces of change that threaten their own wealth and standing? It is in this dynamic of tension - between system thrust and statist response - that the New Nationalism provokes urgent questions for empirical research. The theory presupposes that international development will be geared to the response capacities of rival nations as they struggle, in an increasingly complex and difficult world, to retain a place in the sun. The diagnostic accuracy and the predictive utility of the theory will be proven as nation-states strive to adjust their domestic politics to the harsh dictates of the external order. Theory cannot recommend how national regimes should adjust their strategy, but it can identify the risks that will be incurred if domestic goals are pursued without paying heed to the changing structure of world power. This payoff should not be underestimated at a time when confusion and uncertainty govern the strategic perceptions of so many national actors.

NOTES

(1) An extensive enquiry into system constraints and the submission of national interests to the imperatives of interdependence can be found in many works. Two are of particular value: Edward L. Morse, Modernization and the Transformation of International Relations (New York: Free Press, 1976); Robert Keohane and Joseph Nye, Power and Interdependence (Boston: Little, Brown, 1977).

(2) The success of nation-states in adjusting to external pressure is examined in the title essays by C. Fred Bergsten (ed.), The Future of the International Economic Order: An Agenda for Research (Lexington: D.C. Heath, 1973); and by Peter J. Katzenstein (ed.), "Domestic and International Forces and Strategies of Foreign Eonomic Policy" in a special issue of International Organization, Vol. 31, No. 4, Autumn 1977.

(3) A valuable summary of the trade and investment tactics employed in trade wars is to be found in Charles P. Kindleberger, America in the World Economy (New York: Foreign Policy Association, 1977).

(4) The manipulation of commodity prices, currency values and domestic growth policies is examined in two monographs of Miriam C. Camps: The Management of Interdependence; and "First World"Relationships: The Role of OECD (New York: Council on Foreign Relations, 1974 and 1975).

(5) See the essays collected in Wolfram F. Hanrieder (ed.), Comparative Foreign Policy: Theoretical Essays (New York: McKay, 1971); and The United States and Europe (Cambridge, Mass.: Winthrop, 1974). The symposia survey the maneuvers and diplomatic options exercised by super and middle powers in a world of stable nuclear deterrence.

(6) Robert L. Heilbroner has written two of the best works on "the limits to growth" in an environment of harsh economic constraint: An inquiry into the Human Prospect (New York: Norton, 1974); and Business Civilization in Decline (New York: Norton, 1976).

(7) On the mounting conflict between national interests and the domination of the economic order, see Richard Rosecrance and Arthur Stein, "Interdependence: Myth or Reality?," World Politics, Vol. 26, No. 1, October 1973.

(8) An economic analysis of the political consequences of interdependence appears in two works of Richard N. Cooper, The Economics of Interdependence (New York: McGraw-Hill, 1968); and "Economic Interdependence and Foreign Policy in the Seventies," World Politics, Vol. 24, No. 2, January, 1972.

(9) The difficulties of financing energy inputs and regulating capital outflows is noted in Peter Katzenstein, "International Relations and Domestic Structures: Foreign Economic Policies of Advanced Industrial States," International Organization, Vol. 29, No. 4, Winter 1976.

(10) The failing attempts to integrate the financial policies and the trade maneuvers of the West have been surveyed from different points of view by the contributors to Jagdish N. Bhagwati (ed.), The New International Economic Order: The North-South Debate (Cambridge: M.I.T. Press, 1977). In particular, see the editor's essay, "Market Disruption, Export Market Disruption, Compensation and GATT Reform."

(11) Peter Katzenstein insists, op. cit., that protectionism tends to replace free trade when the leading hegemonial power begins to lose its authority to new rivals. The tensions between the system movers and followers is imaginatively analyzed in Jan Tinbergen (ed.), Reshaping the International Order: A Report to the Club of Rome (New York: Dutton, 1976); and Richard N. Cooper, "A New International Order for Mutual Gain," Foreign Policy. Vol. 26, Spring, 1977.

(12) The pressures exerted on nation-states by system movements are complex but not historically unique. A comparison with previous eras of crisis appers in Daniel Bell, "The Future World Disorder: The Structural Context of Crisis," Foreign Policy, Vol. 27, Summer 1977; and in his Cultural Contradictions of Capitalism (New York: Basic Books, 1976).

(13) A restatement of functionalist theory and political integration has been made by Karl Kaiser, "The U.S. and the EEC in the Atlantic System: The Problem of Theory, "Journal of Common Market Studies, June 1967, pp. 338-425.

(14) Hanrieder's paper in this volume and his essays in note 5 have used slightly different definitions but the quadrant of forces remains true to his terms.

(15) The distinction between Center and Periphery interests has been built into a theoretical model in Johan Galtung, "A Structural Theory of Imperialism," Journal of Peace Research, No. 2, 1971.   A linking of this theory to the MNC appears in Walter Goldstein, "The U.S. Economic Penetration of Western Europe," in Steven J. Rosen and James R. Kurth (eds.),Testing Theories of Economic Imperialism   (Lexington: D.C. Heath, 1974).

(16) I have attempted to survey the data and the literature on the MNCs in an earlier essay, "The MNC and World Trade: The Case of the Developed Economies," in David E. Apter and Louis W. Goodman (eds.), The Multinational Corporation and Social Change (New York: Praeger, 1976).

(17) For an updating of materials on the MNC, see Joseph LaPalombara and Stephen Blank, Multinational Corporations in Comparative Perspective (New York: The Conference Board, 1977); also see Gerard and Victoria Curzon (eds.), The Multinational Enterprise in a Hostile World (London: Macmillan, 1977).

(18) A controversial interpretation of economic nationalism appears in the theoretical essay of R. Harrison Wagner, "Dissolving the State: Three Recent Perspectives on International Relations," International Organization. Summer 1974, pp. 435-466.

(19) See the essay by Harold B. Malmgren, "Trade Policies of the Developed Countries for the Next Decade," in Bhagwati, op cit.; and Wassily Leontieff, et al., The Future of the World Economy (New York: Oxford University Press, 1977).

(20) A distinction between ideological and systemic criticism is advanced in Dennis Goulet, "World Interdependence: Verbal Smokescreen or New Ethic?" Development Paper No. 21 (Washington: Overseas Development Council, March 1976).

(21) For current data on trade aid and development flows, see Werner J. Feld, "Atlantic Interdependence and Competition for Raw Materials in the Third World," Atlantic Community Quarterly, Fall 1976, pp.369-379; and The Changing World Economy (New York: The Conference Board, 1977).

Index

About the Editors and Contributors

WERNER LINK is a Professor of Political Science at the University of Trier where he is also Chairman of the Department. His specific interests are international relations and foreign policy. He took his Ph.D. degree from the University of Marburgh. He is currently the Chairman of the European section of the Committee on Atlantic Studies and is also Chairman of the Board of Trustees of the German Society of Peace and Conflict Research. His publications include: Mit dem Gesicht nach Deutschland. Eine Dokumentation ueber die sozialdemokratische Emigration (with Erich Matthias, (1968); Die amerikanische Stabilisierungspolitik in Deutschland 1921-1932 (1970); Das Konzept der friedlichen Kooperation und der Beginn des Kalten und amerikanischce Gewerkschaften und Geschaftsleute 1945-1975, Eine Studie ueber transnationale Beziehungen (1978).

WERNER J. FELD is a Professor of Political Science at the University of New Orleans. He is author of numerous publications, including Transnational Business Collaboration Among Common Market Countries (1970); Nongovernmental Forces and World Politics (1972); The European Community in World Affairs (1976); Domestic Political Realities and European Unification (with John K. Widgen), (1976); The Foreign Policies of West Euro Socialist Parties (ed.) (1978). In addition, Dr. Feld is the author of more than 50 articles in various journals. He received a law degree from the University of Berlin and a Ph.D. in political science from Tulane University.

JAMES A. CAPORASO received his Ph.D. from the University of Pennsylvania in 1968. Since that time he has been part of the faculty of Northwestern University where he has conducted research on regional integration, international interdependence and global dependency. He is author of The Structure and Function of European Integration (1974); co-editor of Quasi-Experimental Approaches: Testing Theory and Evaluating Policy (1973); and author of numerous articles in journals and books.

ERNST-OTTO CZEMPIEL is Professor of International Relations at the University of Frankfurt/Maine, and Senior Researcher at the Hessische Stiftung Friedensund Konfliktforschung, Frankfurt/Main. He took his Ph.D. from the University of Mainz. His publications include: Das amerikanische Sicherheitssystem 1945-1949 (1966); Macht und Kompromiss. Die Beziehungen der Bundesrepublik Deutschland zu den Vereinten Nationen 1956-1970 (1971); Schwerpunkte und Ziele der Friedensforschung (1972); The Euro-American System (with Dankwart A. Rustow (1976).

ALBINA M. DANN is a graduate student in political science at Carleton University. A native of Montreal, Quebec, she completed her undergraduate studies at McGill University. Her main interests are in the areas of international relations and the comparative study of developing nations.

CHARLES R. FOSTER is executive secretary of the Committee on Atlantic Studies and secretary-treasurer of the Conference Group on German Politics, an independent organization of scholars devoted to the study of German affairs. He has been on the faculties of Indiana University, College of William and Mary, and DePauw University. He has published several articles on German and European politics in scholarly journals.

WALTER GOLDSTEIN is a Professor of Political Science at the Graduate Sschool of Public Affairs, SUNYA. In recent years he has specialized in problems of multi-national firms and international trade policy. He has served as Chairman of the University Seminar on technology and social change at Columbia University. He is author of The Impact of Cross-National Technology on the Uni-national State (1975) and co-author of The Multi-national Corporation vs the Nation State (1975).

WOLFRAM F. HANRIEDER is Professor of Political Science at the University of Calfiornia, Santa Barbara. He has taught at Princeton University, the University of California (Berkeley), and at the Universities of Munich, Braunschweig, and Kiel. His publications include West German Foreign Policy: 1949-1963: International Pressure and Domestic Response (1968), and The Stable Crisis: Two Decades of German Foreign Policy (1970, 1971); and he has edited anthologies on comparative foreign policy and the relations between the United States and Western Europe. He is co-author of a book on West German, French and British foreign policy, to be published later this year.

GUY HÉRAUD is Professor at the University of Pau and also teaches at the European Institute of Advanced International Studies at Nice. Previously he has been Professor of Law and Political Science at the University of Strasbourg. His publications include L'ordre juridique et le pouvoir originaire (1946); L'Europe des ethnies (1963); Popoli e lingue d'Europa (1966); and Les Principes du federalisme et la Federation europeenne (1968).

ROBERT J. JACKSON is a Professor of Political Science at Carleton University, Ottawa, Canada. He is the author of numerous articles on comparative politics and of three books - Rebels and Whips (1968), The Canadian Legislative System (1974), and Issues in Comparative Politics (1971).

JOSEPH LEE was educated at University College, Dublin, the Institute for European History, Mains and Peterhouse, Cambridge. After serving as an Administrative Officer in the Irish Department and Finance and lecturing at University College, Dublin, he was elected a fellow of Perterhouse in 1968. He took up his present position as Professof of Modern History at University College, Cork in 1974. He is the author of The Modernisation of Irish Society, 1848-1918 (Dublin, 1973) and of numerous articles on Irish and German history.

EDWARD L. MORSE is Special Assistant to the Under Secretary of State for Economic Affairs, Department of State. He was Executive Director of the 1980s Project of the Council on Foreign Relations and has taught at Princeton, Johns Hopkins and Columbia Universities. He is the author of Foreign Policy and Interdependence in Gaullist France (1973) and Modernization and the Transformation of International Relations (1976). He has published several articles in scholarly journals and collections of essays.

F.S. NORTHEDGE is a Professor of International Relations at the London School of Economics and Political Science (University of London) and is the Convener of the International Relations Department. His publications include Freedom and Necessity in British Foreign Policy (1972), Descent from Power: British Foreign Policy 1945-1973 (1974), The International Political System (1976). He has written numerous articles and edited several books on international relations.

PANAYOTIS SOLDATOS is Associate Professor of Political Science, Director of the Center of European Studies and Documentation at the University of Montreal and an Associate Fellow of the Institute of European Studies of the University of Brussels. A co-editor of the Journal of European Integration, he is a specialist in international relations, Western Europe, international integration, and Canadian Foreign Policy. Professor Soldatos authored Les données fondamentales de la politique britannique a l'égard de la Communauté européenne" (1973) and "Vers une sociologie de l'intégration communautaire européenne" (1973). He has co-authored "L' harmonisation des législations dans les Communautés européennes" (1976) and has published extensively in various scientific journals.